coaching
KIDS' FOOTBALL

This book is dedicated to Heidi, Aimée and
Chris for putting up with my absolute passion
for football

Acknowledgements

I would like to acknowledge the following people and organisations for their help and support:

Peter Page; Charles Mortimore MBE; the FA; the NSPCC; the team at A&C Black; the staff of Badshot Lea FC, Farnborough Town FC and Reading FC; Sparsholt and South Downs colleges.

Stuart Page

coaching
KIDS' FOOTBALL
Fun, safe and positive football for all ages

Published in 2007 by A & C Black Publishers Ltd
38 Soho Square, London W1D 3HB
www.acblack.com

ISBN 9780713678369

A CIP record for this book is available from the British Library.

Note: While every effort has been made to ensure that the content of this book is as technically accurate and as sound as possible, neither the author nor the publisher can accept responsibility for any injury or loss sustained as a result of the use of this material.

This book is produced using paper that is made from wood grown in managed, sustainable forests. It is natural, renewable and recyclable. The logging and manufacturing processes conform to the environmental regulations of the country of origin.

Acknowledgements
Cover illustration by James Wakelin
Illustrations by Dave Saunders
Cover and inside design by James Wakelin

Printed and bound in Great Britain
by Biddles Ltd, Kings Lynn.

contents

Photograph © Stéphane Rocher 2007

Stuart Page has over 35 years' experience in football, as a player, coach and official. A full member of the FA Coaches Association, Stuart is at UEFA 'A' Licence level and a qualified FA Coach Educator. He also has over 20 years' commercial business experience, having successfully set up and run his own IT Consultancy practice. He currently lectures in sports studies at The South Downs college in Hampshire.

Between 1993 and 2007, Stuart was the Head Coach & Chairman of Badshot Lea FC, based in Surrey, where he was also a Child Protection and Welfare Officer. During his tenure as Chairman, Stuart led the development of the club from very humble beginnings to becoming one of the largest junior grassroots clubs in the UK, running over 25 teams for boys, girls and adults. The club also received the prestigious FA Charter Standard Community Club status and boasts a FA National Volunteer of Year among its management team. From 2004 to 2007, Stuart also coached and managed the Reserve and U18 Youth side at Farnborough Town FC before joining Havant & Waterloovile FC as Head of their Youth Football Academy.

Stuart has also written a complete guide to running junior football clubs called *On & Off the Pitch*, details of which can be found on his website at www.onandoffthepitch.com

Stuart lives in Hampshire with his wife Heidi and their two children, Aimée and Christopher.

Foreword

Charles Mortimore at Buckingham Palace, receiving his MBE in recognition of services to young people in sport (photo courtesy of Charles Mortimore)

I first met Stuart Page in 2000 when his son, Chris, was selected for the Hampshire District Representative team. I immediately recognised Stuart's deep-rooted passion for the game and found him a highly professional and dedicated assistant manager whenever I needed a highly qualified coach to run a District Representative side for me.

Stuart is an approachable and open-minded individual who possesses a sound knowledge of the game. It is of no surprise to me, therefore, that he has written a reference book to help transfer his wealth of coaching experience to teachers and coaches coming into the game. Stuart is also one of those rare people in the game who serves football development without any hidden agendas or for any selfish gain. He is honest and loyal to players, passionate about the game, committed to football's long-term development and firmly behind coaching good practices.

Above all, Stuart has never wavered from his three key principles of the competent coach – for players to be safe, have fun and be inspired. *Coaching Kids' Football* will be a lifelong legacy to his principles, which I totally subscribe to.

It is fair to say that I have enjoyed a long life in and around sport, in particular around young sporting hopefuls. My own footballing career saw me play at the very top of the amateur levels. Once qualified as a PE teacher at Loughborough University, where I captained the football side to the national university championship, I was called up to the Royal Air Force for a two year stint. On leaving the RAF, my 'serious' football career began in earnest with Aldershot in the Football League (South) where I was a prolific goalscorer, notching five goals in one very memorable game against Leyton Orient. I then joined Woking, where the highlight for me was leading them to victory in the 1950 Amateur FA Cup Final at the old Wembley stadium in front of 71,000 spectators. The fact that it was on my birthday, and that the crowd all sang 'Happy Birthday' to me, made it particularly special. As a player, I was fortunate to receive 20 caps for England Amateurs, including being the only ever-present player in a pro/am England side that successfully toured Ghana and Nigeria.

After hanging the boots up, I carried on teaching at Cove School in Hampshire during which time I continued to identify and develop young local talented footballers, helping many become professional players. In 2001 I was immensely humbled yet proud to be rewarded with an MBE in recognition of my services to young people in sport.

I enthusiastically welcome any quality guide to good practice in the game and I am convinced *Coaching Kids' Football* will join the list of 'invaluable' coaching reference. There is a plethora of tactical and technical resources available to coaches, but I found it particularly refreshing to see that *Coaching Kids' Football* directly provides a comprehensive, yet easy-to-follow guide for the inexperienced, non-football-qualified teacher and coach. The book gives invaluable advice on good practice for anyone involved with young footballers, offering comprehensive and sound guides on health and safety, child protection, preparation and delivery of coaching, with plenty of very useful and easy-to-run drills. This is of paramount importance these days because it is these inexperienced teachers and coaches who are responsible for children that are in their 'golden age' of learning and who are our future stars of the game. If we can get the coaching right at this early stage of their development, we might just produce a few more homegrown talented sports stars tomorrow.

CHARLES MORTIMORE MBE

Introduction

Is there anything more delightful than watching children immerse themselves in an activity that is stimulating, progressive and enjoyable, in which they can achieve a level of success that surpasses even their expectations? The delight increases tenfold if the activity also helps to develop good social skills and continued health and fitness.

Although one could list a plethora of activities that fit this category, perhaps the one that springs to mind is sport, and football in particular. Football is enjoyed by hundreds of millions of people around the world, none more so than children under the age of 18. Although the vast majority of children will never play competitive soccer at a professional level, many will play regularly – socially and recreationally – throughout their formative years at school, often at an organised junior club. They will carry what they learn in adolescence into adult life so it is important that anyone responsible for shaping and guiding their learning should do it to the very best of their ability and to the highest standard.

Football is the UK's 'national game'. The most watched sport, it has the greatest number of participants and the most financial investment. It should therefore come as no surprise that the governing body of football in the UK – the Football Association (FA) – is on a constant crusade to implement and maintain high standards of quality and safety. It aims to do this by encouraging, supporting, informing and educating all those involved in football, or considering getting involved.

Did you know that in the UK:

- over three million children aged 10–18 play organised football each week?
- an additional 1.75 million children enjoy a kick-about?
- up to 750,000 adults are involved with these young players?

This book gives you all the information you need to organise successful soccer. Whether you are a passionate volunteer, a schoolteacher or qualified coach, *Coaching Kids' Football* will take you step by step through forming, maintaining and developing young players and teams in a structured, safe and sound manner.

Above all, *Coaching Kids' Football* will provide you with ample guidance and points of reference to ensure that safety, enjoyment and protection are placed highest on the agenda. It aims to help everyone involved in football to develop and implement the necessary good habits and practices to preserve our beautiful national game for centuries to come.

Many children enjoy the game but show no natural skill or ability. These children may be neglected or expected to 'keep up' with the more gifted players by coaches and teachers, which often leads to exclusion. This need not be the case, however, and with good practice parents, teachers, coaches and other organisers can make football fun, healthy, enjoyable and character-building for everyone participating, regardless of their size, age, ability and level of maturity. Coaches can have a dramatically positive influence on a young person's life if, from the start, a policy of good practice, care and attention is adopted.

At club level, the majority of junior football around the world is administered by 'passionate volunteers' who have no formal training or qualifications. When managing children and children's activities, it is vital that adults are well-informed. Sadly, the emphasis on good practice is often overshadowed by the desire to produce 'superstars'. As such, the important aspects of safety, fun, progressive learning and natural development are all too often overlooked, and the needs of less gifted participants neglected. It is therefore vitally important that parents, teachers and coaches are given the same level of help and support that we expect them to give our children. Our children may be the future but it is the adults who guide them and ensure that good practice is maintained and developed.

My involvement in junior/grassroots football has given me the knowledge and experience to get things right, to recognise and act when things are going wrong and to ensure that the children we are responsible for grow up to love the game to which we introduce them. I hope I bring all of this experience and passion to the pages of *Coaching Kids' Football*. As Head Coach I have been responsible for turning enthusiastic parents into competent and qualified coaches. This has not always been easy, as gaining qualifications is not high on everyone's priority list. However, this issue is quickly resolved when I ask parents how they would feel if someone who refused to obtain appropriate coaching and child protection qualifications was responsible for coaching their children.

In this book I have included chapters on risk assessment, preparation for activity and actions to take in the event of emergencies. There are plenty of coaching drills relative to age, level of maturity and physical development, with additional guides on how to make football educational without losing the fun, enjoyment and health and safety aspects. The book is designed to cover the many situations coaches, parents and teachers will face as they help guide football-loving children's journeys to adulthood. I hope you enjoy the book and will derive benefit from it for many years to come.

STUART PAGE

part 1

AN INTRODUCTION TO COACHING

chapter 1
LAYING THE FOUNDATIONS

There is no doubt about it: a safe and enjoyable coaching and playing environment, such as a well-run football club, can have a profound and positive social impact on its members and the local community, especially the children. It can create, shape and develop a good sense of responsibility, respect, care and welfare among all.

The good practice guidelines that clubs and schools now have to adopt, particularly if they are to achieve FA Charter Standard status, do have a knock-on effect on young players who have to embrace and uphold the standards or risk being excluded. I have seen the most street-hardened and aggressive individuals, who show an alarming disrespect and disregard on day one, do a U-turn in their attitude and general demeanour after a short while, displaying a real passion for their club and care for others within it.

Codes of conduct at most clubs make provision for all user groups: teachers, coaches and managers, players, officials, parents, members and spectators. These common-sense guidelines lay out the behaviour and values expected by the club, and exist to protect the interests of the club and its members. They are there to say to anyone wishing to buck the rules that they are not welcome and that their social skills and levels of respect are unacceptable. So, even before a ball is kicked members sign up to a set of rules that will ensure a high level of behaviour.

Players, especially at youth ages, can display a quite shocking lack of respect towards whatever is provided for them and those who provide it. Yet these attitudes can quickly be changed for the better through the pleasure of playing a game they love, the discipline of teamwork and the benefits of hard work. It is the thought of having these withdrawn because of their poor levels of respect, commitment and general social graces that really wakes up disruptive and misbehaving individuals.

A controversial point maybe, but it is arguable that a well-run football club has a greater social impact than perhaps a school classroom or workplace might, in so much as the environment is recreational, sociable and is there to fuel fun and enjoyment in a sport its participants and members love.

It is clear that the FA – through its Charter Standard Awards – sees the important role played by well-run football clubs in shaping good social environments. The Charter Standard Community Club and Charter Standard School accreditations are the highest awards for quality and standards available. These are given to clubs and schools that have all the attributes to become the focal point of football within the local community. Such organisations also provide links and exit routes for players, and volunteers of all ages and abilities, while setting the standards to which all other local clubs and schools aspire.

As a well-run football club brings so many benefits to its members and the local community, it is essential that those involved in running the clubs lay a good, solid foundation. They need to establish a baseline of discipline and rules that clearly lays out the high standards of behaviour, attitudes, ethics and values expected of members and participants, but which also maintains maximum fun, enjoyment and safety.

FA Charter Standard Quality Accreditations

The Charter Standard Scheme is a best practice guide that sets standards of coaching, administration and child protection for clubs, schools and colleges working with young people. As a benchmark for quality, it will improve the playing experience for all. To be blunt, my advice to parents seeking a safe and quality-driven environment for their children is to find a club that has attained the FA Charter Standard accreditation. This will ensure your child is being coached in an environment where a stringent child protection policy is in place, and where all coaches are qualified in coaching and emergency first aid and have attended the FA Child Protection workshop. To find out more about FA Charter Standard accreditation and how your school or club can qualify, visit the FA's website at www.thefa.com.

So, such ground rules are vital and should be in place before anyone at your club kicks a ball. This way, everyone – and rules are not just for players but for members, officials, coaches, parents and other spectators alike – knows what is acceptable or unacceptable behaviour, and is aware of the potential consequences if the rules are not adhered to; put simply, this will be the withdrawal of benefits for those who do not respect the code.

There are a number of organisations who can give guidance on good practice and goal-setting, as well as offering financial support to community projects. I have detailed some of these organisations later on in this chapter. Firstly, here are some guidelines on areas you should consider when drawing up your standards of good practice, based on my experiences.

Attitude and Ethics

The basic principles to uphold are fair play and overall participation, not the result of the game. There is nothing unhealthy about wanting to win – football would be nothing without its competitive nature – but there are ways and means of expressing oneself in the face of victory or defeat.

Players

Players need to learn self-discipline and the fundamentals of fair play to ensure that everyone gets the most out of playing football. Though young people might regularly see examples of bad behaviour from players at football grounds and in televised matches, they need to learn that such behaviour will not be put up with at any level! The FA and other football governing bodies take a dim view of such antics and so should you.

Self-Control

- Getting angry and/or crying when losing or having lost are unacceptable, even if only directed at oneself. This only has a negative impact on other people and should be kept in check
- Taking out one's frustrations on someone else is also unacceptable, be it a team-mate who has made a mistake or a referee whose decision one disagrees with
- You should remember that verbal abuse, telling someone that they are no good or making threatening remarks are every bit as harmful as physical bullying or intimidation
- Spitting at any other person is disrespectful, disgraceful and insulting
- Any form of physical contact intended to cause harm to another person must not and will not be tolerated.

Fair play

- Targeting individual opposition players, either physically (e.g. by persistent deliberate fouling) or verbally (insults/threats) to try and gain advantage is against the spirit of fair play and must not be tolerated
- 'Play-acting', e.g. feigning injury to try and get an opposition player sent off or falsely reporting an incident to an official, is as bad in its own way as a professional foul or a verbal insult

- Players should act respectfully towards their opponents, shake hands with them at the end of the game and say 'well done', whether this be accepting defeat graciously or showing empathy in victory. Remember that without the opposition, there could be no game.
- Players should not brag or gloat in victory, especially in front of the opposition.

Coaches

It is essential to appreciate that a coach is not just there to teach young people football skills, and that coaching staff have a duty of care to the youngsters in their charge. Do not underestimate the influence coaches' actions could have on young people and how they conduct themselves. Below are common mistakes for coaches to avoid and alternative actions, followed by a list of competencies you should adopt for a code of conduct that ensures better coaching and mentoring at your club.

Coaching Principles – Dos and Don'ts

- Do show commitment to the team, but channel energy positively, even when things are not going well on the pitch
- Don't argue with officials if you disagree with their actions – this will only legitimise this kind of behaviour in your players' eyes
- Do try and establish a good relationship with your players from the beginning and be as warm and approachable as possible so that they will respect you
- Do set down basic ground rules, but don't 'lay down the law' or be too inflexible in your approach
- Do make sure you are consistent – don't break your own rules or make exceptions for certain individuals
- Don't withdraw players from activities for disciplinary reasons, as isolation of individuals will probably cause more problems
- Do use positive reinforcement within the structure of your activities to discipline players who break the rules
- Don't be hard on players who 'under-perform'
- Don't over-promote or overuse skilful players, or place them on a pedestal
- Do use praise, but only with justification
- Don't shame less talented players by making an example of their mistakes or by comparing them to more skilful individuals
- Do consider that players of differing skill levels can play together
- Do remember that every young person is an individual who might be more or less sensitive to criticism, constructive or otherwise
- Do take note that if you pick on a particular young person and criticise them

publicly, others might see this as a licence to continue to abuse or ridicule the individual when you are no longer there

■ Do listen to your players – if you need to change things at half time or mid-season, allow the team to have their say and make constructive and positive comments to you and one another in an objective way. They might think of something you hadn't considered.

Coaching competencies

Below are some of the attributes a good coach needs to tailor activities to everyone's advantage, based on FA guidelines, with some advice and examples of positive outcomes from my experiences:

Responsive

I've had teams where individual players have told me that they find a certain skills exercise too hard, for example. Consider whether the activity you're doing is beneficial depending on the age and skill level of all the participants and adapt accordingly. Be a problem-solver; innovate and improvise.

Accountable

Remember that as well as the responsibilities of a duty of care to your players and looking after your own interests, you owe it to your colleagues to reflect the effort they put into assisting you with activities. Your role is as much about the continued development of football in the community as it is teaching football skills, so a lot of people are relying on you.

Courageous

You are there to set standards, so be brave and aim high! Make the quality of your coaching raise the bar for performance; do it without fear, as long as you feel it's right for the game and is realistically attainable by everyone involved with what you're trying to achieve. Be open to new suggestions, and make sure you give credit and assurances to encourage players and other people at your club to take responsibility. You'll be amazed at how a few words of positive encouragement will motivate people to help you. I couldn't have developed the clubs I've been involved with through my individual efforts alone.

Inclusive

Within reason, rotate your squad! Reflect your players' enthusiasm and commitment by giving them an equal share of opportunities. Be careful to reassure 'dropped' players that they are still in with a shout and encourage them to train hard with the rest of the team. If a player is on the subs' bench, try to make sure you use them.

Passionate

You are a role model – if you love the game and show it, you will make the young people in your charge do the same.

Organised

Use your knowledge in a focused way and have goals to achieve standards. Make sure when you are coaching that the players understand why you are doing an activity and what you are aiming to achieve. Don't use complicated language, especially when explaining things to younger players. Remember that children will have been inspired to play football by watching their favourite teams and players without necessarily knowing all the rules.

Code of Conduct

Hopefully you will now have a good idea of the kind of standards and codes of practice required by a well-run football club. Taking this one step further, the FA has published codes of conduct that apply to all footballing organisations, from Premiership clubs down to the grassroots. They set out positive standards to adhere to, and reject negatives.

There are FA codes for coaches, players, officials and other relevant parties, including parents and spectators. For more details, see www.thefa.com.

Anti-Discrimination and Equal Opportunities

Football is the UK's national game; today we are as ethnically and culturally diverse as any nation. Instilling a sense of equality into young people at the earliest age possible is therefore essential. Naturally, the FA takes the lead in promoting equal opportunities (see box on page 9), but they are not the only organisation involved with educating people on the need for equality of opportunity at all levels of football and assisting community projects. In this section I have detailed some useful sources of help, information and inspiration when you are considering diversity and equal opportunities at your club.

FA Anti-discrimination Policies

The FA's Football for All education and training programme includes a three-hour workshop looking at generic equality and diversity issues for grassroots football and those making decisions, along with a diversity competence training strategy across the whole of football.

The FA's policies state that football belongs to, and should be enjoyed by, everyone equally. Their objective is to eliminate discrimination whether by reason of gender, sexual orientation, race, nationality, ethnic origin, colour, religion or ability, and to encourage equal opportunities. Such policies should be at the heart of every club's, school's or community's activities.

For more details on the FA's specific policies in this regard, see www.thefa.com.

Sporting Equals

In 1998, the Commission for Racial Equality and Sport England launched Sporting Equals, an initiative that works to promote racial equality in all sport throughout England. Sporting Equals cooperates with sport governing bodies and umbrella organisations to ensure that ethnic minorities are accorded fair representation at the very top of organisations, and right down to the grassroots, and addresses issues of race within sport.

The policy of Sporting Equals has similar goals to those of the FA. As well as advocating full participation regardless of race, it aims to change established attitudes in governing bodies and sports providers, and to highlight cultural diversity, recognise it and celebrate it through sport. For more information, see www.sportingequals.com.

Sport for Communities

Run by Sporting Equals in partnership with the Department for Culture, Media and Sports (DCMS), and with local authority sport and leisure agencies, Sport for Communities helps develop integrated sporting activities in inner-city communities, including travellers and migrants, not just settled ethnic minority communities.

A number of case studies are published on the Sporting Equals website as downloadable documents for reference. See www.sportingequals.com for further information.

Show Racism the Red Card (SRTRC)

Part of the Football Against Racism in Europe (FARE) network, SRTRC was set up as a registered charity in 1996 to raise the issue of racism through high-profile campaigns with professional footballers of all races and nationalities playing in the UK. As well as organising events with community groups, SRTRC provides educational materials such as magazines and posters of high-profile teams; these are free of charge (except for the cost of postage) for single items, and at a nominal cost for bulk orders. An educational DVD or video for children of primary and secondary school age featuring top players and managers is available with an education pack, also at cost – this is £20 at time of publication of this book.

The main website contains details primarily for organisations in England. For more information, see www.srtrc.org. See below for details of SRTRC in other parts of the UK.

Scotland

Show Racism the Red Card Scotland run workshops for young people through-out Scotland; recent high-profile participants in the Scottish campaign include Neil Lennon and Nigel Quashie. Partners include Sport Scotland, Learn Direct Scotland and the Scottish Executive. Features of the site include a section for reporting acts of racism and sectarianism, which from 1 September 2006 in Scotland has become a criminal offence punishable by a 10-year match ban. For more information, see www.thredcardscotland.org.

Wales

Information for Welsh organisations is available as a link from the main SRTRC website and includes Welsh-language pages. See www.srtrc.org/wales for more information.

Kick It Out

Kick It Out was established in 1993 and, like SRTRC, forms part of the FARE network. Funded by the FA, the FA Premier League, the Football Foundation – the largest charitable organisation for grassroots football in England and Wales – and the Professional Footballers' Association (PFA), Kick It Out takes its message into schools and youth organisations and uses high-profile names from the top of English football – David James and Rio Ferdinand have been campaign poster-boys – to raise awareness. With goals such as tackling issues of racial abuse and harassment in the amateur game – both adult Sunday-league and kids' park football – Kick It Out helps forge links between 'family clubs' to allow them to share their experiences with other communities and clubs through support for initiatives, educational material, anti-racism workshops, and even partnerships. The organisation's media relations machine can even be made available for big events. See www.kickitout.org for more details.

South Asians in Football

Despite thousands of young sub-continental Asian fans and young amateur foot-ballers, their under-representation in the professional game is staggering. At the time of writing, there are two professional south Asians in the Premiership; in 2005, it was reported that there were only 10 south Asians in Premiership academies. Kick It Out's campaign seeks to redress the balance and dispel myths – such as the misguided notions that 'Asians are only interested in hockey and cricket' or 'Asians are too busy with religious commitments' – and asks where problems still remain. High-profile supporters include Zesh Rehman, a product of Fulham FC's 'Search for a Star' initiative in south London communities. Rehman cites the 'chicken and egg' situation of a shortage of south Asian role models like himself to inspire young Asian players to higher achievement, hence his involvement.

Kick It Out also supported the *Asians Can Play Football* report authored by Jas Bains, chair of the National Asians in Football Forum, in 2005. Its initiative invites participants in the amateur game to report on progress at their clubs and any obstacles that are still being encountered by young Asians.

IFA Football for All

Since 1998, the Irish Football Association (IFA) has worked with the Northern Ireland Community Relations Council, Sports Council Northern Ireland, and Amalgamation of Official Northern Ireland Supporters' Clubs to address the issue of sectarianism in football, through its Football for All initiative. Football for All is also assisted by the EU Programme for Peace and Reconciliation. The principal aim of the initiative is to ensure that football in Northern Ireland is inclusive to all members of society in the province, and its policy spells out the right to participation regardless of perceived cultural identity, political affiliation or religious beliefs. The IFA's vision is that the game of football should become the most popular and inclusive sport in Northern Ireland. A 10-point plan outlines details for finding a common strategy with police, local authorities and com-munity groups to eradicate sectarian graffiti, chants and abuse wherever the occur in football.

The IFA has also always sought to ensure that its training courses are cross-community and its national team is a fair representation of different social backgrounds.

For more information, see www.irishfa.com./grassroots/football-for-all.

Diversity Champions

It is estimated that between two and ten per cent of the population is homosexual, yet openly gay players, coaches and other people involved in the national game are virtually non-existent. Stonewall, the gay rights charity, has developed a Diversity Champions award scheme, which encourages employers across the UK to work with them to fund initiatives that afford homosexual people fair representation at different levels of organisations. Manchester City FC are the first Premiership football club to sign up to the scheme, and hope to encourage more gay fans and staff to the club through the aims of Diversity Champions, and create a 'family club' atmosphere where everyone feels they can enjoy football without worrying about small-minded prejudice. You should consider introducing an anti-homosexuality section to any codes of conduct at your club to encourage participation of people of all sexual orientations, be they coaches or young people. For more information, see www.stonewall.org/workplace/32.asp.

Summary

I have been in and around football for many years as a parent, coach, manager, teacher and player. In this time, I have come to fully understand the critical importance of 'quality, standards, codes of conduct, responsibility and under-standing'. These are not simply words without meaning, but rather important ingredients that ensure 'everyone' in the 'team' fulfils their obligations towards a healthy, happy, safe and enjoyable experience within football. These ingredients must never be compromised, regardless of your role or involvement. As mentioned at the beginning of this chapter, a well-run club or school team can have an immense positive impact on the social attitude and actions of those involved – perhaps even more so than school or the workplace. The environment you help to create is exciting, fun and caring, educational, inspiring and challenging – all things that help positively shape a young person's movement through life.

As a teacher or coach, continually reflect on your role and the manner in which you deliver your education or coaching. As a parent, always consider the impact you are having on your child in the responses and advice you give them. Is it positive? Is it helpful? Is it relevant to the betterment of your child's development?

As a player, simply show respect for everything that is provided to you – the taxiing to games and training, the coaching given, the financial support and facilities provided. Finally, I urge all spectators to be fair, rational and respectful – towards the officials, the players, the opposition and the organisers. Enjoy the experience of watching the game and seeing the development of those involved.

If all these ingredients can be blended correctly, the basic foundation is set for a fabulously enjoyable experience for everyone involved.

chapter 2
CHILD PROTECTION AND SAFETY

The majority of children who do sport do so in a safe and helpful atmosphere, with genuine support from coaches, volunteers and other club staff. But for the small minority of children who are abused during sporting activities, the picture is very different.

The sports community recognises the need to protect children from individuals who might abuse positions of trust. In your work as a sports professional, there are a number of steps you can take to help safeguard children and young people. You can also play an important role in protecting children who may be experiencing abuse in other areas of their lives.

As discussed in chapter 1 with regard to equality and fairness, it is vital that you develop a robust code of conduct to deal with issues of child protection, abuse and neglect. If your club receives any public funding, you are obliged to have such policy in place.

I have detailed below some of the issues you must consider and include in this process. Firstly I have outlined definitions of abuse and neglect you should strive to prevent, and then discussed issues of staffing and facilities, and other considerations, that should constitute your club's policies and code of conduct.

Further information on child protection and safety issues discussed in this chapter can also be found at:

- www.thefa.com
- www.nspcc.org.uk
- www.thecpsu.org.uk
- www.crb.gov.uk.

Child Abuse and Neglect

According to the Children Act of 1989, a 'child' is any young person under the age of 18. This raises issues of responsibility, self-awareness and a young person's maturity. For example, a young person may feel ready to engage in sexual activity when they reach the legal age of consent at 16, though still legally a child.

FA Child Protection Policy

As the foremost organisation in England, the FA takes the lead on child protection. It is positive and proactive in giving guidance to organisers at every level of football for the provision of a safe playing environment. It outlines the same 'duty of care' as discussed in the previous section on codes of conduct. The FA's approach is designed to create high standards of care from an ethical viewpoint.

The FA's courses and associated materials are developed in conjunction with the National Society for the Prevention of Cruelty to Children (NSPCC); each course is quality-assured. All FA courses have child protection content as an ethical constant alongside organisation of activities and coaching.

For more information, visit www.thefa.com.

Therefore some situations you could encounter might be less 'black and white' than they first appear. Let's consider definitions of abuse and neglect, with some examples you might witness in practice:

Abuse

Child abuse can be defined as physical, emotional or sexual harm perpetrated by someone on a young person directly. Such examples might include:

- Physical bullying or maltreatment, including hitting and shaking, or forcing an individual to perform to an inappropriate level, e.g. making a young person do far too much physical exercise for their development
- Inappropriate sexual behaviour for the abuser's self-gratification, such as unwarranted physical contact with a young person, exposing them to pornography or making lewd remarks
- Humiliation or unfair 'singling-out' for criticism during sporting activity.

Neglect

Neglect is the systematic failure of those in authority to adequately account for a young person's psychological or physical needs, or failure to prevent them from coming to harm. Examples of neglect could include:

- Failing to provide sufficient warm clothing during activities on a cold day, or not allowing liquid refreshment on a hot day
- Exposing a young person to undue risks of abuse or injury

- Failing to act on signs of possible abuse by others
- Not providing adequate access to other means of help and support for young people with problems.

Responsible Adults

In this section, we need to look at how to recruit and manage staff and volunteers, ensure they are well versed with rules and requirements, detail those requirements and also consider other factors where adults and young people come into contact in the course of their involvement at your club.

Staff and Volunteer Recruitment

It should go without saying that you must be extremely vigilant and thorough when it comes to interviewing and taking on staff and volunteers. It is important to note that any adult taking a role at your club must:

- have a clear role, be it a head coach, assistant coach or other
- have substantiated qualifications for the specific role
- if possible provide references from previous employers/organisations
- have Criminal Records Bureau (CRB) disclosure/clearance (see box)
- sign up to your club's child protection policy in full
- attend a quality-assured course organised by the FA

CRB checks

The Criminal Records Bureau was approved in law by the Police Act 1997 and established in practice in 2002, before which many activities in which adults supervised children were not subject to screening. The CRB is an executive agency of the Home Office, administered by a private firm, Capita. However, civil servants carry out the confidential checks process itself.

The CRB is designed to be a 'one-stop shop' to search for current and spent convictions, cautions, reprimands and warnings; this can include data on the Police National Computer, and databases for the Department for Education and Skills (DfES) and Department of Health (DH), as necessary. The report returned by the CRB is known as a 'disclosure'.

At the time of publication, for positions of paid employment, a fee of £31 is applicable for a standard disclosure and £36 for an enhanced disclosure.

The standard disclosure is usually all that is required for most roles – enhanced disclosure tends to be required for roles in which the individual in question will be the sole person in charge of young people (e.g. a Scout or Guide leader). For volunteer roles, no fee is payable.

While an individual may apply for paperwork to gain a CRB disclosure, all completed documentation must be handled by the organisation – in other words, you must liaise with the CRB to obtain the disclosure on behalf of anyone you need to clear for a role at your club. It is not possible to clear yourself for a role if you are, say, a self-employed coach, though it is possible to get clearance if registered with an agency who will deal with the CRB on your behalf. This situation is less likely to arise if you are looking to work with an established club.

There is a code of practice that anyone receiving disclosures must sign up to, to ensure that the information provided is used fairly and in the right context. Someone applying to work with young people who has a conviction, e.g. for credit card fraud, does not necessarily need that conviction to be made common knowledge by your club if it is irrelevant to the role. Only if they were in a role that could involve misappropriation of club funds or those of a disabled child in their care might this be deemed 'in the right context', and even then it is required to be disseminated on a 'need to know' basis only. Personal information within a disclosure must in any case be stored responsibly and disposed of within six months of receipt.

For more information on CRB checks, please see www.crb.gov.uk.

As we discussed in chapter 1, children and young people are suggestible, so a good example must be set by anyone working at your club. This means that they should not use abusive, obscene or otherwise bad language, should not smoke or consume alcohol in the presence of young people in their care, or use drugs; nor should they encourage or glamorise any such habits. In turn, any responsible person at your club must not tolerate the above at any time, either by a young person or another adult. There can also be issues of a sexual nature to deal with. Something 'innocent' may inadvertently become an enquiry; similarly, incidences of criminal behaviour could occur unbeknownst to you. The robustness of your code of conduct to deal with such matters will provide a clearly drawn line of acceptable and unacceptable behaviour by anyone in your club.

Physical Contact and Sexual Abuse

Physical contact – between a responsible adult and a young person or between one young person and another – must only occur in the strict context of sports activity and/or skills improvement, or when administering first aid.

Positioning a child to demonstrate the correct way to conduct an exercise may involve physical contact from the adult teaching the skill. This should only occur in full view of other participating young people and only when necessary. The adult in question must explain the context of what they are doing both to the child and others present. There is never a reasonable excuse for touching a child's genital area, buttocks or breasts. When supervising disabled children, it must be decided before any activities take place what contact with the child is or is not acceptable with the child's parents/carers (and preferably the child themselves) and to gain strict permission.

In the case of injury to a child, any incidence must be officially recorded and parents informed of any treatment given, which may or may not have involved physical contact. As with demonstrating exercises, any contact must be in strict context, avoid sexually sensitive areas of the child's body and be explained to the child. Any incident where an adult inadvertently hurts a child – for example, a coach refereeing a practice match might run with the play and accidentally knock over a standing child they haven't seen in their path – must also be officially recorded and reported to parents. For more information on first aid and medical attention, see chapter 3.

Any incident that occurs where a child reacts in a certain unexpected way or misinterprets an activity, where the adult in question's behaviour is blameless, should also be officially reported and parents informed. An example of this could be a child's apparent sexual arousal by innocent physical contact.

The golden rule for physical contact is that if the young person can do something without you needing to touch them, there should be no contact. It's as simple as that.

Sexual Contact

Any relationship or sexual contact between an adult over the age of 18 and young person under the age of 16 is regarded as a criminal act and should be treated as such by your club if it occurs. See later in the chapter for more information on dealing with this.

As I mentioned at the beginning of this chapter, lines can be blurred where a 'child' under 18 but over the age of 16 is involved. Your policy must prohibit any relationship between a young person and anyone with a position of authority within your club, even if the young person is 16 or over. The conflict of such a personal relationship with the duty of care for young people in their jurisdiction makes such a position of authority untenable, especially considering the possible emotional immaturity of young people in their care.

For example, if a relationship involved a male coach and a teenage girl, she might feel obliged to partake in acts of a sexual nature she would otherwise not be happy to, in order to keep 'in favour' with the coach in question. Also, if the coach has singled out this individual for such attention, she might feel 'special' and therefore use this to try misguidedly to enhance her own status with her peers. For the coach's part, he might demonstrate favouritism that conflicts with the system of equal opportunity at your club, e.g. picking the girl for every game and not offering the same opportunities to play to other young people.

Among children themselves at your club, sexual relationships are quite likely to occur, just as they are at school or anywhere else where young people spend time together. Any outward behaviour, even holding hands and kissing etc., should be strongly discouraged during group activities and games, if only because it is unfair on other young people and can be discomfiting and distracting to them. Try pointing this out to individuals involved and ask, would they like it if someone else were doing it when they wanted to get on with an activity? In my experience, this is always a firm 'no'!

How to act on signs of abuse

The FA has produced a series of extremely helpful flowcharts on what process to go through when you are alerted to potential abuse of a young person. For a detailed look at these charts, please refer to FA course material or visit the www.thefa.com.

Below is a simple checklist of what to do or provide at your club to deal with signs of abuse effectively:

- Ensure that there is a rigid framework in your code of conduct for recording and acting on allegations or signs of abuse (see sample record form on page 22)
- Take all allegations or signs of abuse extremely seriously
- Listen carefully to everything a young person tells you, even if the details are hard for you to deal with, or if you find it a shock or difficult to believe at first hearing
- Remember that young people are all different and will act and react differently in any given situation
- Within context of allegations or signs of abuse, involve other responsible adults at your club with your investigations and reporting, e.g. if a girl alleging abuse

feels more comfortable talking to a female member of your club staff, ensure that she has the opportunity to do so

- Do not confront or involve in an inquiry any adult at your club that is the subject of allegations
- Keep a lookout for any non-verbal signs of abuse e.g. unusual bruising on a child's body or uncharacteristic behaviour from a particular child that could hint at untoward activity.

On the field

You must make staff aware of the need to be vigilant when supervising groups of young people, particularly if the pitch/field is public or in a publicly accessible area. Make sure that a list of children is always handy for a group so that you can keep tabs on which child is where. Younger children are naturally more demanding, easily distracted and naïve, so a smaller child-to-adult ratio is needed for younger children.

Another useful system is 'buddies', more about which is explained in the 'out and about' section later in this chapter.

If equipment is in use, you should check that children know how to use it properly and that it meets suitable standards of safety (see section on risk assessments on pages 26–8). For example, ensure that goalposts are sufficiently anchored to the ground; do not let children hang from the crossbar of the goal, etc.

Other adults

There will be times when there will be other adults, such as photographers or journalists, present at training sessions or matches for perfectly legitimate reasons.

You must ensure that these reasons are definite, and that any visiting journalist or photographer is aware in advance of your club's code of conduct, health and safety issues and so on. If you are hiring them for their services, for example to use video footage for training purposes, you should check beforehand that the staff/company are reputable.

All photographing, videoing or interviewing (as appropriate) should be supervised, and no individual children should be separated from a group without the strictest appropriate context, and certainly this must not be done out of sight.

Consent forms must be completed and signed by a parent or guardian in advance of any photographing or filming that occurs, for every child appearing, and detailing the specific event in question, and forms officially kept. (See page 22 for a sample consent form.) Should any parent object, the child in question must not appear in any photography or filming. If this is unavoidable, the event must not be filmed.

Parents are naturally proud of their children – they will want to take photographs and, with video cameras so affordable and even mobile phone technology now so readily available with cameras, in many cases wish to film their kids playing football. In these cases, parents should be given clear advice on when and how it is appropriate to gain this kind of footage. This can be included in your code of conduct for parents and children (see later in this chapter for more on this).

Sample Consent Form for the Use of Photographs or Video (Parents and Children)

(*Club or organisation*) recognises the need to ensure the welfare and safety of all young people in sport.

In accordance with our child protection policy we will not permit photographs, video or other images of young people to be taken without the consent of the parents/carers and children.

(*Club or organisation*) will follow the guidance for the use of photographs, a copy of which is available from (*insert name*).

(*Club or organisation*) will take all steps to ensure these images are used solely for the purposes they are intended. If you become aware that these images are being used inappropriately you should inform (*club or organisation*) immediately.

I (*parent/carer*) consent to (*club or organisation*) photographing or videoing (*insert name*).

Date ....

I (*name of child*) consent to (*club or organisation*) photographing or videoing my involvement in (*sport*).

Date ....

Out and about

Contact details

A child's registration with your club must include taking and carefully storing contact details. The first and obvious reason for this is in case of an emergency where an individual's parents need to be informed of an injury, for example.

The other reason is lateness. If you are at an away game and are delayed, policy should be in place to notify parents of any changes to plans or details at the earliest opportunity. Contact details should also contain a 'fallback' option in case the first point of contact is unavailable. This can be another relative of the child, or even parents of another friend within the same club/team.

Another excellent idea for disseminating changes of plan quickly and more easily for you is to set up a 'phone pyramid' whereby you call two people, who call two more people and so on until everyone in the pyramid in descending order has been contacted. You should ensure that everyone in the list has given their full consent to be added and that the pyramid can be adapted at short notice in case of trouble contacting one of the 'principal' names. For example, Steve Smith in the sample pyramid on page 24 could be uncontactable for some reason, so contingencies must be in place to work around the pyramid differently to contact everyone.

Time changes

A key to this part of club policy is to publish clear times for regular training sessions and try to stick rigidly to these so that parents can plan when to collect their children. Where fixtures or times do have to change, you must let parents know at the earliest opportunity.

Another advantage of the contact details is in cases where a parent is unable to collect their child at the expected time. In these situations, you *must* contact the parent in question to explain the situation. Under no circumstances should you allow another parent to drive the child home instead, unless express permission has been given by the parent when you've contacted them for other arrangements to be made. Even then, this should only happen if they are known to the child and trusted by the parent. You should also not allow staff members (including yourself) to drive a young person home unless it is absolutely necessary and is the only option available. Even then, this should only be with the parent's prior consent. You should also never allow anyone to leave any young person in a vehicle unattended. Remember that you have a duty of care to a child until they are safely delivered back to their parents.

Other contacts:
Maria Gomes (Coach) – 01010 888444
Darren Martyn (Coach) – 01010 789123
Demarion Alexander (Chairman) – 01010 655555

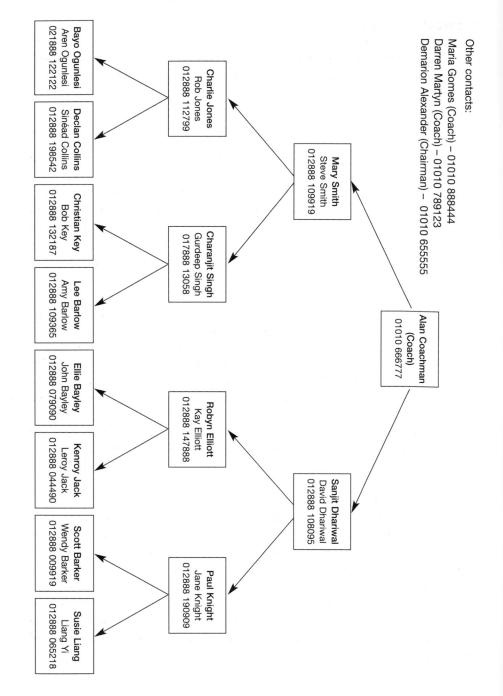

Alan Coachman (Coach) 01010 666777	

Mary Smith Steve Smith 012888 109919

Sanjit Dhariwal David Dhariwal 012888 108095

Charlie Jones Rob Jones 012888 112799

Charanjit Singh Gurdeep Singh 017888 13058

Robyn Elliott Kay Elliott 012888 147888

Paul Knight Jane Knight 012888 190909

Bayo Ogunlesi Aren Ogunlesi 021888 122122

Declan Collins Sinéad Collins 012888 198542

Christian Key Bob Key 012888 132187

Lee Barlow Amy Barlow 012888 103365

Ellie Bayley John Bayley 012888 079090

Kenroy Jack Leroy Jack 012888 044490

Scott Barker Wendy Barker 012888 009919

Susie Liang Liang Yi 012888 065218

Transport needs

You should take into account particular requirements of any young people in your care when on the road. Suitable vehicles/access may be required for some disabled individuals, for example, or medicines looked after, e.g. asthma inhalers kept with the child.

Supervising groups of children

As we've already discussed, it is vitally important to know where all the children are in your care, and that they are safe. This can become even more difficult when you are in a strange town or away from your familiar 'home' environment, particularly when you have a number of highly excited children to look after. Make sure that you have sufficient staff numbers to cope with this change of environment and that you are placed in such a way as to see all the children (for example, at opposite ends of a 'crocodile' of children walking down the street). Disabled children should also be given adequate supervision according to their needs.

Another good system is 'buddies' where each child has a partner, whom they seek out whenever you call out 'Buddy!' Best friends will usually be with their buddy already, but more mobile children within the group will be able to seek theirs out elsewhere and confirm that all are present and correct. Where there is an uneven number, ensure that the odd number makes up a group of three with two buddies to find. If a disabled child is on the trip, even though they will be given extra supervision, do include them in the buddies system so that they are an inclusive part of the group.

Though this is a fun way of keeping tabs on numbers, and should be treated as such, you should also explain to children why the game is being played, and make sure that they don't suddenly decide to change buddies halfway through the trip!

In the changing rooms

You are likely to need changing facilities at your club. Separate provision must be made for male and female changing, supervised by two adults of the same sex as the young people concerned. Staff should not change or shower at the same time in the same facility as the children.

Young people can be sensitive about changing or undressing in front of their peers. If unhappy about doing so, they should not be forced to shower or undress in the changing rooms. In these situations, it is advisable to encourage the young person to shower as soon as they get home and to think about their personal hygiene in this way.

You should keep an eye out for any bullying or teasing directed at a young person when changing or showering, and take action to stop this happening in accordance with your code of conduct.

As with transport, it is necessary to ensure that disabled people have sufficient facilities. If a parent or carer is required to help with changing, the same gender rules apply as for staff. For example, a mother changing her son will need a changing room separate from other males. This should be handled sensitively so that the child does not feel too 'segregated'.

Club facilities – Health and Safety Risk Assessment

Your duty of care towards young people and issues of neglect extend to facilities and equipment. Regular risk assessments should be completed, using the same key criteria each time. An example of a completed risk assessment form is on pages 29–30; a blank form for you to use is in the appendices on pages 180–1. First, here are the criteria and sections you should include in detail.

1. The venue, date, and name/position of person carrying out the assessment should be clearly marked. This person must be of some authority within your organisation.

2. Check all areas that will be used for activities, such as hard-standing areas, fields etc. Check for any obstacles or other hazards (litter, broken bottles, dog waste) or other factors likely to be a risk to safety. Make a note of any obstructions, hazards, and action taken.

3. Any equipment, fixed or portable, must be looked at carefully. Goals are likely to be the most important of these, so:

- check condition, i.e. for corrosion. Rust can weaken some metal structures, but more often it can cause overlying paint to peel, crack, and/or expose bare metal which then corrodes further, with the risk of abrasion or laceration if contact is made
- check anchorage to ground. Weighting is important, no matter how large or heavy goal structures are, or if they are fixed or moveable. Portable goals should be weighted with chain anchors when in use to prevent forward movement or collapse, and locked up in a secure place/position when not in use to avoid unauthorised use/misuse. Larger, fixed goals should be anchored more securely, preferably into the ground. Check anchorage by exerting *reasonable* force forwards, backwards and sideways on the posts, and downwards on the crossbar

- ensure hooks for attaching nets to goals are made from plastic, so that they are flexible on contact. Metal cup hooks are dangerous and should be removed and/or replaced
- check goals are as manufactured, not customised in some way that compromises safety, e.g. cut down to a smaller height

Make a note of any offending items of equipment removed or replaced, or further action to take.

4. Are your players all registered fully with up-to-date emergency contact details (see more on page 23)?

5. Check players all have the following, or have been briefed to bring it with them:
- trainers or soft-studded Astro shoes (if playing indoors or on Astroturf)
- studded boots if playing on grass (trainers are only acceptable if the ground is completely dry)
- shinpads. Many players don't consider it necessary to protect their shins, which are only one mistimed tackle away from being painfully skinned, bruised or even broken without shinpads. Even if the level of contact isn't as great as a full match, ensure that young people in your club get used to wearing shinpads at all times when training
- a drink. While clubs and schools provide water bottles, these are more often than not passed around several players, contain old water from last week, and look pretty sorry for themselves besides, covered in mud from being chucked around on the ground during training, picking up germs from the ground. Encourage your players to bring a bottle – with their name on it, preferably – containing a non-fizzy drink for their own consumption. Make sure it's kept upright during the session, ideally in a carry-tray so it's away from the ground completely.
- a towel. Even if they cannot be persuaded to shower (see page 25), at least they can dry themselves off if it's been teeming down with rain.
- a change of clothing. Even if the young person is wearing the correct kit, quite often they won't have brought anything dry or clean to change into afterwards. Not only is sitting around in wet and dirty clothes not great for a child's health, it hardly helps their parents' car upholstery either. Encourage the wearing of a tracksuit so that it can be put back on after the game or training. You might even want to get a club training kit for all the kids to wear as well a playing kit for the game itself.

6. Emergency Points – is there sufficient access for emergency vehicles in the event of an accident? Any parked cars should be away from entrances from the road and to playing areas

7. Ensure safety information, basic first aid advice (see also chapter 3) and emergency telephone numbers are on display around the club. Note down what is/was missing and what action has been/will be taken

8. Sign and print your name.

Other help with setting up child protection policy

As well as the FA (see box), other organisations are very active with child protection, which will help you develop and implement your own policy.

The FA and Child Protection

A number of FA workshops and reference materials are available to your staff members, and even keen parents, either free of charge or at reasonable cost. At the time of writing, a copy of the FA's Child Protection Guide is £11.75, and a workshop costs around £15 per person. Some county FAs even subsidise these workshops on behalf of smaller organisations.

For more on FA Child Protection initiatives, see www.thefa.com.

NSPCC

The FA/NSPCC Child Protection Helpline (0808 800 5000) is available 24 hours a day for both adults and children to speak to someone, confidentially and anonymously if necessary, about concerns they might have. You should make this number available to members, their parents, and anyone working at your club.

Within the NSPCC are NSPCC Consultancy Services, who provide help and advice through a number of useful publications, one of which is the *Firstcheck* information pack.

Firstcheck

The *Firstcheck* pack is described as the 'health check' for your club; a specially designed check-up and assessment of whether your club is sufficiently child-friendly and safe. Divided into four user-friendly sections, the pack is designed to be cross-referenced to allow you to establish your policy and develop partnerships

Risk assessment form

Venue/Date: **Yew Trees FC, Hornchester – 18/08/07**
Name/position: **A. Coachman (Head Coach)**

Playing/Training Area

Are areas free of dangerous obstacles? Is area fit and appropriate for chosen activity? (Tick appropriate response.)

Yes   No   ✔

Outline any hazards and detail what action was taken or will be taken:

Debris and bottles from trespassers left on pitch, now disposed of.

Goalposts/other equipment

Are goalposts safe and appropriate for the activity? Yes   No   ✔

Outline any unsafe equipment, who may be at risk and what action was taken:

Offending metal cup hook removed from crossbar and replaced with plastic net hook; Sharp, rough rust patch on left-hand upright sanded down and repainted.

Players

Is the emergency contacts/medical register completed and up-to-date?

Yes   No   ✔

Outline current state and what action was taken:

Charanjit Singh's family moved house last week, so Charanjit updated me with new address and his dad's new mobile number for emergencies.

Is all the players' attire appropriate and safe for chosen activity?

Yes   No   ✔

Outline any unsafe equipment/attire and any action taken:

Kenroy Jack has lost his shinpads; found suitable replacements for now in equipment store and asked Kenroy to try and buy a new pair for next week.

Emergency Points

Can emergency vehicles access areas safely and without obstacle?

Neighbouring house has permission to use the club car park, but owners have parked on entrance slip,,so have asked them to park car in the car park itself.

Is telephone working?

Yes, tested it by calling my own mobile number, which worked.

with parents, other organisations outside your club, and the young people themselves, to implement it successfully.

Once a framework is in place, NSPCC Consultancy Services can check the contents of your policy and make suggestions or advise of changes needed.

At the time of writing, *Firstcheck* is available at a cost of £20, direct from the NSPCC. Any consultancy work on your individual policy is subject to a fee negotiable with NSPCC Consultancy Services. See www.nspcc.org.uk for more details.

Child Protection in Sport Unit (CPSU)

The CPSU was formed in 2001 and is a partnership between the NSPCC, Sport England, Sport Scotland, the Sports Council for Northern Ireland and the Sports Council for Wales. Its formation followed the 2000 National Action Plan for Child Protection in Sport.

The CPSU is set up to be a first point of contact for advice on any issues of child protection. This could be help with vetting of staff, or provision of briefing papers and training to leading figures in your club. They provide a support and communication network to help your club leaders liaise with other sporting organisations on child protection issues.

As discussed, you might have a role in rehabilitating a child who has suffered abuse or neglect. The CPSU can lend support to this process.

For more on the work of the CPSU, see www.thecpsu.org.uk.

chapter 3
HEALTH AND WELFARE

First Aid

Did you know that by giving up just three hours one evening you could obtain a qualification in emergency first aid that is valid for three years and might save a life? It is common sense for people to have some knowledge of first aid. Knowing the basics is invaluable and may be called upon in everyday life, not just when you are associated with football. So the obvious recommendation is, 'get qualified'.

Taking a basic emergency first aid course is simple. There is no test or written exam. You just need to demonstrate to the instructor that you have taken on board their tuition and can put it into practice. I can truly say that every first aid course I have been on has been fun and enjoyable, and has given me the opportunity to make new friends. Each time I have learned new things and refreshed the areas I had forgotten. The FA can provide contacts at your local county FA who will be able to organise an appropriate first aid course for you, or you can contact organisations who run the courses (see boxes below and on page 34).

The British Red Cross

The Red Cross run a number of courses that will be relevant to working at your club. At the end of each course, a credit card-sized certificate for wallet or purse is awarded, which is valid for three years.

The basic course, the Red Cross's most popular, is run over seven hours, and covers subjects such as cardio-pulmonary resuscitation (CPR) (see page 39–40 for more details), shock (see page 51) and choking (see more on page 41). The practical course is 14 hours in duration, and also covers situations where you are dealing with people living with conditions like asthma (see page 58) and diabetes (see more on page 59). The Standard certificate course is 28 hours and covers a large number of situations and conditions such as crush injuries, hypothermia (see page 55) and even poisoning. It is the most advanced course available to the public, and includes a good deal of theory, though assessment is continual throughout the course and there is no written exam.

For more on British Red Cross courses, see www.redcross.org.uk or call 0870 170 9222 (select option three).

St John Ambulance

The relevant courses run by the St John Ambulance are likely to be the basic first aid course and Activity First Aid. Unlike the Red Cross course, the basic St John Ambulance course does not cover CPR. The activity-based course is aimed specifically at people working with groups of young people over the age of 10. In addition to subjects covered by the basic course and other intermediate courses, this covers managing casualties outdoors, emergencies in public, conditions relating to extremes of temperature, e.g. hypothermia (see page 55) and heatstroke (see page 53), recognition and treatment of low blood sugar (see page 59), and the role of the first aider in a group setting.

St John Ambulance courses are subject to a reasonable cost. See www.sja.org.uk for more details.

It is important that coaches are qualified in all aspects of dealing with young people. These days, the FA coaching certificates at all levels incorporate child protection workshops and first aid. Additionally, qualified coaches have the opportunity to join the FA Coaches Association, which comes with professional and public liability insurance cover as part of your membership. Again, it is common sense that you are adequately insured against any claims of negligence that might be made.

At my local club we also ensure that at least one other regular attendee at the matches – such as an assistant manager or parent – is qualified in first aid and child protection. To encourage participation, the club even pays for them to do the courses. The number of people at our club qualified in first aid is growing, from players in the senior sides to parents and officials. It should not be a hard slog trying to get people at your club to attend a first aid or child protection course. Common sense says they should attend.

The bottom line is you never know when you are going to need your emergency first aid skills. In a sport like football where there is a high probability of injury, knowing the basic emergency first aid procedure could stop a serious injury getting worse and even save a life!

Keeping a record

If an injury or incident occurs, you must make an official record and inform the child's parents, even if the child is fit enough to continue an activity after treatment.

First aid procedures: basic conditions and treatments

As I've said, there is no substitute for a professional first aid course, but as a handy reference to photocopy and take onto the field with you, the following pages contain the most common problems and conditions you might have to deal with. You should always be well prepared, so ensure that you keep a comprehensive first aid kit bag on the sidelines at all times in case of emergency (see box below). And if you use any of the contents – make sure you replace them!

Equipment for the first aid bag

- Small waterproof zip bag
- Protective disposable gloves (latex)
- Sterile gauze squares
- Disposable bag for gloves, gauze squares etc.
- Butterfly skin closures
- Small spray bottle containing sterile water for wound cleansing
- Disposable ice pack
- 7.5cm elastic adhesive bandage to hold gauze pad(s) in position
- Roll of 2.5cm zinc oxide tape for gauze fixation in cases of bleeding
- Plasters (various sizes)
- No 9. Bandages (x 2) for profuse bleeding

These contents are occasionally subject to advisory or legislative updates, so you should check FA guidelines regularly at www.thefa.com.

The Primary Survey (DRAB/C)

Danger

Before you assess the casualty, make sure that neither you nor the casualty is in danger. In most cases, the game or activity will stop immediately so that this can be done safely.

Response

If the casualty has been knocked out or appears unconscious, check by shouting something like, 'Can you hear me?' and shake them gently by the shoulders if necessary. Is there a response?

- **Yes** – summon help onto the field or activity area as required, but do not move the casualty. Treat any condition that has arisen and monitor pulse and breathing continually until further medical assistance arrives.
- **No** – immediately call for help. If the casualty is on their back, open their airway. If they are in a different position and it is unavoidable, turn them gently onto their back and then open the airway.

Airway

Place one hand on the casualty's forehead and tilt the head back. Use two fingers of the other hand to lift the chin, so that the tongue is moved away from the back of the mouth (see below).

Breathing/CPR

Look to see if the casualty's chest is rising and falling; place your head close to the mouth to listen for breathing or to sense the heat of the casualty's breath on your own skin (see illustration on page 37). Are they breathing normally?

- **Yes** – place them in the recovery position (see page 38).
- **No** – you should begin cardio-pulmonary respiration (CPR) (see more on

pages 39–40); if the casualty is breathing but not in a normal or regular way, you should still begin CPR. (For example, the condition *agonal breathing* can occur after a sudden cardiac arrest, resulting in sudden irregular gasps.)

Note

Historically, the C in DRAB/C stood for *Circulation*, but in some revised modern protocols, this step stands for *Cardiopulmonary resuscitation* or, more simply, *Compressions*, which is effectively artificial circulation.

Once oxygen can be delivered to the lungs by a clear airway and efficient breathing, there needs to be a circulation to deliver oxygen to the rest of the body. This can be initially assessed in a number of ways, including a pulse check, breath being inhaled/exhaled, rising and lowering of the chest, pale skin showing colour returning, and a warming up of the body temperature.

The recovery position

A casualty should only be placed in the recovery position if they are breathing normally:

■ Turn the casualty onto their side

■ With the head to one side, tilt the chin forwards to open the airway. Rest the casualty's cheek on their hand if necessary. If you suspect the casualty has a spinal injury, *do not* tilt the chin. Instead, place your hands on either side of their face, using your fingertips to lift the jaw gently and open the airway. This is known as the jaw thrust technique

■ Ensure that the casualty is positioned so that they cannot roll forwards or backwards

■ Keep a close eye on their vital signs (i.e. pulse and breathing) to make sure their condition is not deteriorating

■ Depending on the nature of their injuries, turn the casualty over to the other side after 30 minutes.

Cardio-pulmonary respiration (CPR)
In the unlikely event that there is no one else present to call 999, you should give one minute's CPR to the casualty *before* calling 999 *if they are pre-pubescent*. With older children who have reached puberty, call the emergency services first and then administer the CPR. If you are unsure, for the reasons discussed in the section in chapter 2 on physical contact, it is inappropriate and unnecessary to check. In such cases, proceed with the 'adult' version of CPR detailed below.

Children (up to puberty)
First, administer *rescue breaths*:
- Make sure that the airway is opened as described on page 36 for 'Response'
- Pinch the nose and seal your lips around the child's mouth
- Looking along the chest to see that the chest rises, blow gently into the lungs, ensuring that you do not completely empty your lungs
- When the chest has risen, stop blowing and allow it to fall
- Repeat four times (so, five rescue breaths in all), then check for circulation.

Then, administer *chest compressions*:
- Depending on the size/age of the child, place one or two hands in the centre of the chest. It should be possible to determine the correct place without removing any of the child's clothing
- Keeping your arms straight, use the heel(s) of your hand(s) to depress the chest one-third of its depth, and then release, leaving the hand(s) in position after the compression
- Press 30 times at a rate of 100 compressions a minute (so a series of compressions should take 18 seconds), then give two rescue breaths as described above.

Continue the pattern of 30 compressions/two rescue breaths, without breaking the sequence, until further assistance arrives.

Older children/adults

First, administer *chest compressions*:

- Place the heel of one hand in the centre of the chest. Place the other over the top of it and interlock the fingers of both hands
- Keeping your arms straight and your fingers away from the chest, depress the chest by 4–5cm, then release, leaving the hands in position after the compression
- Press 30 times at a rate of 100 compressions a minute (so a series of compressions should take 18 seconds).

Then, give two *rescue breaths* as described for younger children, above. Continue the pattern of 30 compressions/two rescue breaths, without breaking the sequence, until further assistance arrives.

Choking

There are two forms of choking, mild or severe depending on the kind of obstruction. The below instructions relate to treatment of both children and adults so should cover all ages of young people you may have to treat.

Mild obstruction

The casualty will be conscious and breathing, and may be able to cough, and communicate distress through crying or speaking. It may be that they are eating or drinking too fast, or at an inappropriate time, e.g. when they are actually performing an activity.

Look immediately in the mouth for obvious objects causing obstruction and remove them. Encourage the young person to keep coughing to clear the obstruction, and keep them calm in case they panic and cause themselves harm. Keep monitoring the casualty to ensure their symptoms do not worsen.

Severe obstruction

In this case, the casualty will not be able to breathe, cough, cry and speak. If left unassisted, they will eventually become unconscious.

First, administer up to five *back blows* – quick, sharp blows between the shoulder blades with the heel of your hand. Immediately check the mouth and remove any obvious obstructions.

If the obstruction has not been cleared, give up to five *abdominal thrusts*. To perform abdominal thrusts (also known as the *Heimlich Manoeuvre*), stand behind the casualty and wrap your arms around their middle. Holding one wrist with the other hand, place the clenched fist of the other hand between the navel and the bottom of the breastbone, and pull inwards and upwards. Check the mouth quickly after each thrust.

If the obstruction does not clear after three cycles of back blows and abdominal thrusts, call for an ambulance. Continue the cycle of blows and thrusts until help arrives or you have removed the obstruction. If you successfully remove the obstruction and the casualty is unconscious but breathing normally, place them in the recovery position (see page 38).

Limb fractures

There's a fair chance, with the rough and tumble of football activities and young people with growing bones, that fractures will occur. While you cannot actually treat the fracture itself, there are other things you can do to assist and calm the casualty:

- Keep the young person calm and reassure them that they will be OK
- Persuade them to stay still, and do not move them yourself unless strictly necessary
- Support the limb with your hands to prevent any movement that will cause more damage and/or distress
- If there is bleeding, carefully press a clean pad over the wound to control the flow of blood. When you have done, bandage carefully around the wound
- If you suspect a broken arm, improvise a sling to support the arm close to the body (for guidance on how to make a sling, see box below)
- If you suspect a broken leg, it is important to try and immobilise the leg by placing a pad between the knees and ankles, then gently but firmly bandaging the injured leg to the uninjured one, improvising a splint
- Call for an ambulance
- Continue to reassure the casualty and watch out for signs of shock (see page 51). If the casualty falls unconscious, use the DRAB/C sequence and/or recovery position (see pages 39–40 and 48)
- Do not give the casualty anything to eat or drink in case they need an urgent operation on the fracture.

Making a sling

Note! This advice does not replace proper first aid training – there are various ways of making an emergency sling such as this; great caution should be exercised.

- Take a clean square lint bandage. Your first aid kit should have one specifically for this purpose. Fold diagonally into a triangle
- Slip the bandage underneath the arm (see illustration A at foot of page 43) so that one corner is at the neck and opposite shoulder from the arm to be slung
- Bring the lower part up so that it cradles the arm in a secure position as close to the body as comfortably possible. Be careful not to cause pain and distress to the casualty when elevating the arm (see illustration B)

■ Bring the second corner up to the neck on the same side of the arm and fasten carefully to the other side of the sling behind the neck with safety pins (illustration C).

Bleeding

The most likely cause of bleeding in young people in your care will be through a cut, graze or scratch e.g. from falling on to a hard playing surface or colliding with another player. Occasionally, a more serious injury may cause severe bleeding that you will need to contain until it can be given hospital treatment.

Minor bleeding

- Hygiene is essential. Wash your hands thoroughly and dry them. Cover any cuts, grazes or scratches on your own hands, and wear disposable gloves – these are as much to protect you from infection as the casualty
- If dirt is in a cut, place it under running water (if possible). Pat dry with a sterile dressing or other clean lint-free material. If there is a foreign object lodged in the cut, you will need to follow a different procedure (see box below)
- Cover the wound temporarily with a sterile dressing or other clean lint-free material, then clean the area around the wound with soap and water, patting dry carefully with another clean material
- Cover the wound completely with a sterile dressing or sticking plaster.

Objects in wounds

If a large object is embedded in a cut that cannot be removed by washing with clean water, proceed as follows:

- Leave the foreign object in place
- Apply firm pressure either side of the object
- Raise and support the wounded limb or part, being careful not to cause undue pain or distress to the casualty
- Lay the casualty down in case of shock (see more on shock on page 51)
- Gently cover the wound and the object with a sterile dressing
- Build up layers of padding around the object until the level of padding is higher than the object, so that you can cover the object without placing pressure on it
- Bandage over the object
- If bleeding is light, seek medical attention at an A&E department for further treatment; if bleeding is severe, call an ambulance and treat the casualty for shock.

Severe bleeding

- Again, wash your hands thoroughly and dry them. Cover any cuts, grazes or scratches on your own hands, and wear disposable gloves
- To stem the bleeding, apply direct pressure to the wound with a pad (e.g. a clean lint-free cloth) or fingers until a sterile dressing is available
- Lay the casualty down in case of shock (see more on shock on page 51)
- Raise and support the wounded limb or part, being careful not to cause undue pain or distress to the casualty
- Bandage the pad or dressing firmly so as to staunch the flow of blood, but be careful not to bandage legs or arms too tightly and cut off circulation to the toes or fingers
- If blood seeps through bandage, do not remove it, but apply another one over the top – if the blood continues to seep through the second bandage, only then should you remove the bandages and go through the process again
- Call for an ambulance
- Treat for shock (see page 51).

Nosebleeds

Nosebleeds are usually caused by rupturing of the tiny blood vessels in the nostrils. There are a number of ways that nosebleeds can occur during football activities – an impact on the nose from a ball at close range, or blowing the nose and sneezing (both common in hay fever season), for example.

Some young people will be more predisposed to nosebleeds than others, so you should make a note of any child who is particularly susceptible. If the nosebleed is heavy, it can cause a dangerous loss of blood for the young person. Should this occur, follow the below procedures, but transport or send the child to A&E according to club rules (see chapter 2, pages 23–5, for details on conduct when transporting children).

Note! If a heavy impact to the head causes a nosebleed where the blood is thin and watery, it is highly likely that the skull is fractured and fluid is leaking from around the brain. For more on skull fractures, see page 48.

- Sit the casualty down and ask them to tilt their head forwards, so that the blood will drain from their nostrils
- Ask the casualty to pinch the soft part of their nose and keep it pinched, breathing through their mouth instead (which will also have a calming effect). *Do not* tilt the head back, as blood may run down the throat and induce vomiting or choking. Make sure the casualty does not cough, swallow, spit or especially sniff, as this may disturb blood clots forming in the nose
- After 10 minutes, ask the casualty to stop pinching their nose but keep their head forwards. If blood continues to flow, repeat the procedure for a further two periods of 10 minutes. If the bleeding continues after 30 minutes, transport or send the child to A&E according to club rules (see chapter 2, pages 23–5, for details on conduct when transporting children). Ensure the child maintains the head-forwards position in transit
- If the bleeding has stopped, clean gently around the nose with clean, lukewarm water. Should the bleeding restart, begin process of treatment again
- Tell the casualty to rest quietly for a few hours and not take part in any activities that might cause the blood clots in the nose to be disturbed.

Concussion

Concussion is caused by a blow to the head where the brain, which has some room to move within the skull, is 'shaken'. There follows a brief period of impaired consciousness where some function is lost, usually only a few minutes – a classic example of this is a boxing match where a fighter is 'knocked out', can barely stand and seems confused about where they are and what is going on, but in fact is then sufficiently *compos mentis* to give a press interview shortly afterwards. Concussion is very common in contact sports generally.

Recovery is usually complete, but some other symptoms may occur post-recovery, such as:

- mild, generalised headache
- dizziness and nausea
- no memory of event that caused concussion or events immediately it.

If recovery is quick, ensure that they continue to rest, and make sure someone monitors their pulse, breathing and level of response to ensure that they do not deteriorate, indicating a worse head injury (see also information on skull fractures on page 48 and cerebral compression on page 50). If symptoms continue or worsen, or if any other ill effects begin to show such as blurred vision or excessive sleepiness, seek medical attention.

Skull fracture

This injury hit the headlines in 2006 when goalkeeper Petr Cech of Chelsea collided head first with the boot of Reading's Stephen Hunt in an English Premiership game. Great concern was shown at the time of the injury, and Cech's rapid recovery (albeit to play in a rugby-style protective cap) surprised many experts.

There are few more serious injuries you will ever have to face than a skull fracture. Any head wound or injury should quickly be assessed to see if a possible fracture has occurred. Signs to look out for are:

- wound or bruise on the head
- soft area or depression on the scalp
- clear fluid or watery blood emerging from either ear and/or the nose
- blood in the white of the eye; bruising around either or both eyes
- distortion or lack of symmetry in the head or face
- impaired consciousness; progressive deterioration in level of response.

Remember that your job in this case is to ensure that the casualty is breathing and stable so that an ambulance can be called and emergency treatment sought. There are two possible courses of action to take, depending on the condition of the casualty:

Conscious casualty

- Help the casualty lie down
- Make sure you *do not* turn the neck in case of a spinal/neck injury
- Control any bleeding of the scalp by applying careful pressure around the wound (see pages 44–5 for more on treating bleeding)
- Call an ambulance
- If there is discharge from the ear, place a clean pad or sterile dressing over the ear and lightly secure it with a bandage. Do not plug the ear
- Keep a close eye on the casualty's breathing, pulse and their level of response (i.e. keep them talking) until the ambulance arrives.

Unconscious casualty

- Open the airway using the jaw thrust technique and establish vital signs using the primary survey techniques described on pages 36–7, then follow the DRAB/C process as necessary
- Call an ambulance
- If the casualty is in a position that makes the jaw thrust impossible or an open airway difficult to maintain, and if you have assistance on hand, use the log-roll technique to get the casualty into the recovery position (see box on page 49).

Log-roll technique

This technique is so called because it involves a number of people all rolling the casualty carefully and in a controlled manner at the same time like a log.

All working together, the team of people slowly turn the casualty over simultaneously, avoiding any bending, twisting or other movement that might further damage the spine or neck and cause paralysis.

Cerebral compression

This injury generally occurs when an impact to the head leads to pressure on the brain, with damaged brain tissue swelling or blood from the brain causing pressure within the skull. It is extremely serious and is most likely to occur in the same situations as a fractured skull (see page 48). However, unlike a fractured skull, the symptoms or effects of cerebral compression are not obvious immediately and can occur hours or even days later.

As with a skull fracture, the conscious casualty will display a deteriorating level of response, which could be accompanied by a change in personality/behaviour such as irritability or disorientation, and may then fall unconscious. Other signs to look out for *in conjunction with the lack of response* are:

- slow, laboured breathing
- slow but strong pulse
- unequal pupil size in eyes
- high temperature/flushed face
- weakness and/or paralysis down one side of the face or body.

If you are aware that one of the young people in your club has had a knock to the head for any reason in recent days (whether or not it was playing football), you may want to consider if it is sensible for the child to participate in any risky activity where a worse injury may occur.

Your first action should be to call an ambulance. Then treatment should be as follows:

Conscious casualty

- Make sure that they are in a comfortable position, preferably with the minimum of movement, and reassure them
- Monitor and record their level of response, pulse and breathing at regular intervals until the ambulance arrives.

Unconscious casualty

- Open the airway using the jaw thrust technique and establish vital signs using the primary survey techniques described on pages 36–7, then follow the DRAB/C process as necessary.

Try to maintain an open airway with the casualty in the position they were found, even if that makes the jaw thrust difficult to perform.

Shock

Shock can occur as a result of serious injury and is usually due either to blood loss from an injury preventing vital organs (including the brain) functioning properly or the body's reaction to psychological upset from fear or pain. Shock will almost always occur to a greater or lesser degree, but the symptoms may be missed if other obvious injuries are being attended to. Shock may also occur as a delayed reaction, hours afterwards in some cases, so you should remain vigilant when treating a casualty. You should watch out for:

- Pallid complexion or cold, clammy skin
- Rapid, weak pulse
- Quick, shallow breathing
- Feeling sick or actual vomiting
- Yawning or sighing.

In extreme cases, the casualty may fall unconscious. In this instance, you should place them in the recovery position and monitor them closely (see page 38 for more on the recovery position). If the casualty remains conscious, you should treat as follows:

- Give plenty of comfort and reassurance
- Lay the casualty down, raising and supporting their legs so that blood will flow to vital organs (see illustration below)
- Do not allow the casualty to get too hot or cold. Use a blanket or coat to keep them warm, but do not smother them
- Refrain from giving them food or drink, even if they ask for it
- Regularly check the casualty's breathing and pulse. If they stop breathing, follow the DRAB/C process (see pages 36–7)
- If the casualty complains of difficulty breathing or begins to vomit, place them in the recovery position (see page 38).

Heat exhaustion

The chances are that you'll be supervising activities at your club in the summer months, particularly during the summer holidays when kids are out and about all day long in strong sunshine. You should therefore be aware of the risks of heat exhaustion, heatstroke (see page 53) and sunburn (see page 54), as the effects can be debilitating and dangerous.

The main cause of any heat exhaustion you encounter is likely to be dehydration. Excessive sweating on hot days can leave the body short of the water it needs to function. Despite the regular reminders we hear of the danger of excessive salt intake, it should be remembered that salt in the right quantities is essential to organ function. The loss of salt through sweating is also a factor in heat exhaustion.

Symptoms to look out for are:

■ Headache
■ Pallid complexion or cold, clammy/sweaty skin
■ Rapid, weak pulse
■ Quick, shallow breathing
■ Dizziness/confusion
■ Feeling sick or actual vomiting
■ Loss of appetite
■ Muscle cramps in the abdominal wall, arms or legs.

You need to cool the casualty down and replenish their bodily fluids before any dangerous deterioration takes place in their condition. Treat as follows:

■ Help the casualty if necessary to a cool place out of the sun
■ Lay the casualty down, raising and supporting their legs so that blood will flow to vital organs
■ Give the casualty plenty of water but discourage a large intake at once to avoid bloating which may cause vomiting
■ Give the casualty a weak salt solution, mixing one teaspoon of salt with a litre of water. Again, do not let the casualty drink this too suddenly in case of a nauseous reaction. Provide plenty of encouragement and assistance if necessary, as younger children in particular will probably find drinking the solution unpleasant
■ If the casualty's responses continue to deteriorate, place them in the recovery position (see page 38) and call an ambulance. Monitor vital signs and be prepared to give CPR if necessary (see pages 39–40)
■ Even if the casualty makes a quick recovery, encourage them to seek medical attention in case of a relapse or any other ill effects.

Heatstroke

This condition is seen when the body's ability to regulate temperature (by the thermostat in the brain) is adversely affected. This can be caused by overexposure to the sun on hot days or as a result of the effects of heat exhaustion (see page 52). The body becomes dangerously overheated and functions can begin to fail. Note: Though there may be a causal link, heatstroke should not be confused with heat exhaustion, as some of the symptoms are different.

Symptoms to look out for are:

- Headache
- Hot, flushed/dry skin
- A full, bounding pulse
- Dizziness/confusion/discomfort/restlessness
- A rapid deterioration in the level of response
- Body temperature over 40 degrees Celsius (104 degrees Fahrenheit).

You need to cool the casualty down before any further deterioration takes place in their condition. Treat as follows:

- Move the casualty as fast as possible to a cool place and remove as much of their outer clothing as possible (see page 19 in chapter 2 for guidelines on appropriate contact with young people in doing this)
- Call an ambulance
- Wrap the casualty in a cold wet sheet or, if no sheet is available, fan them and sponge them with cold water. Continue to do this until their temperature drops to 38 degrees Celsius (100.4 degrees Fahrenheit), then wrap them in a dry sheet or some other clean material, as available
- Keep monitoring their vital signs until the ambulance arrives. If their temperature begins to increase again, repeat the cooling process, as above
- If the casualty becomes unconscious, use the DRAB/C sequence (see pages 36–7) and be prepared to use CPR (see pages 39–40). If the casualty is unconscious but breathing normally, put them in the recovery position (see page 38) and monitor their breathing closely until the ambulance arrives.

Sunburn

Overexposure to sunlight is commonplace, particularly in Britain where the weather can change rapidly from rain to shine and cold snap to heatwave, leaving people unprepared. There is also still a certain degree of laissez-faire and ignorance amongst some people about the real dangers of prolonged solar exposure, fuelled in part by the body-beautiful images of tanned celebrities seen in magazines and on TV.

You should make young people and their parents aware that they should be protecting themselves from sunburn, and/or making such provision available at your club. For times where children are outside for long periods, a high-factor sun cream is essential. If the sun index is high enough in summer to cause sunburn after only one hour, a low-factor cream may not be enough if the young person is out all day in the sun. It should also be remembered that even thin, high cloud lets through enough ultraviolet light from the sun to cause sunburn, not just direct sunlight.

As well as sun cream, encourage young people to wear a hat if possible, as this will protect their scalp, neck and face from increased exposure. It will also reduce the risk of heatstroke (see page 53).

Symptoms of sunburn are:

- Reddened skin, often made more obvious by 'strap marks' when clothing is changed or a white mark e.g. a patch of skin revealed when the young person removes their watch
- Stinging, soreness or burning pain of affected area
- Blistering of the affected skin in severe cases (may occur a while after exposure)

Treatment is as follows:

- First and foremost, get the young person out of the sun, preferably indoors
- In minor cases, cover the affected areas with thin clothing or a towel
- Cool the skin by sponging, bathing or asking the casualty to take a 10-minute shower with cool water
- Encourage the casualty to take regular sips of cold water
- If necessary on minor sunburn, apply – or ask the casualty to apply as appropriate – after-sun cream or calamine lotion to the affected area
- If the burns are severe and/or blistering occurs, seek medical advice or attention
- Keep an eye out for symptoms of heatstroke that may result from prolonged exposure (see page 53).

Hypothermia

Hypothermia is a condition arising when the body cannot keep its core temperature high enough to function properly. Severe cases are unlikely to occur at your club, but the early stages of hypothermia might occur if you are taking football sessions outside on particularly cold days, especially if the weather is also inclement and/or windy . You should ensure that young people in your care wear sufficient clothing for the temperature and climate (e.g. rain) and have sufficient fuel (i.e. food) to keep them going. More layers of thin clothing are better than fewer thick layers, as they trap more air for better insulation. Hats are also a good idea, as around 20 per cent of bodily heat loss is through the head. And keep them moving, as exercise generates heat!

Symptoms to look out for in mild to moderate cases of hypothermia are:

- Goose pimples pronounced on the skin
- Bouts of shivering, becoming more violent as condition worsens
- Grogginess/confusion
- Lack of concentration or deterioration in level of response
- Slow, shallow breathing
- Slow, weak pulse

If severe hypothermia sets in, shivering stops, irrational behaviour such as stripping off layers of clothing may occur, and eventually the casualty will fall unconscious, but you will have spotted the danger signs and acted before it could ever get to this stage! To treat for signs of the cold:

- Take the young person out of the cold/wind/rain
- Put them in dry clothing if wet and add more thin layers to help warming – the main torso/trunk area is most important as this is where the core temperature is maintained
- Give them a hot drink and something to eat, preferably also hot. Do not be tempted to give any young person a 'medicinal' brandy or other 'warming' alcoholic drink. No one of any age should be given alcohol to try to counter the effects of cold, as alcohol causes dilation of peripheral blood vessels, increasing heat loss
- Do not wash hands of feet under hot water to warm them as this is likely to cause blistering and chilblains
- Make sure the young person is supervised to ensure that their condition does not worsen.

Insect Stings

On summer days, the air is usually thick with insects. When it comes to stings during days like this, most you are likely to experience will be from wasps. Most people dislike wasps, and many will panic or lash out in fear if they encounter one. Unfortunately, wasps are quite persistent when they pick up the scent of sweaty bodies and can react to flapping arms and swatting, which is when stings can occur. Less commonly, bees or hornets may also sting.

Your responsibility is to treat the sting with a minimum of fuss and arrange any medical treatment. You should also keep an eye out for any severe allergic reaction to the sting – known as anaphylaxis (see page 57), which is rare but can be fatal. The visual signs of the sting will be:

- swelling at site of sting
- redness around the sting.

To treat the casualty:

- Reassure the casualty and calm them down as much as possible. Younger children will probably be more distressed through the sheer unfamiliar pain of the sting
- If the sting is visible, brush or scrape it off the skin. To avoid stinging yourself, use the blunt side of a knife or a credit card to do this. Don't use tweezers or any other implement which may squeeze more poison from the sting into the body or push the sting further in
- Place ice or other cold pack to the sting to bring the swelling down and soothe the pain, if possible raising and supporting the affected part
- Monitor very closely any stings in and around the mouth (or even throat), as swelling can restrict the airway or even block it. In this case, try and give the casualty an ice cube or lolly to suck, or cold water to sip, that will reduce swelling. If breathing does become difficult, seek medical attention immediately
- If breathing is impaired and the sting is not in the mouth or throat, this may be as a result of allergic reaction. Other symptoms of allergy are swelling to the face, neck, tongue, mouth or lips (usually unconnected to the sting site), or widespread rash. An ambulance should be called immediately. See following page for more on anaphylaxis.

Severe allergic reaction – anaphylaxis

Fortunately, anaphylactic reactions are rare, but can onset suddenly and be fatal. The most likely causes you will encounter are allergic reactions to stings or reactions from the accidental consumption of nuts in young people who have nut allergies. For more on identifying anaphylaxis and its causes, see http://www.anaphylaxis.org.uk/.

Symptoms of anaphylaxis are:

- impaired breathing, ranging from a tight chest to severe difficulty breathing, or wheezing/gasping for air
- swelling to the face, neck, tongue, mouth or lips, or widespread rash
- puffiness around the eyes
- anxiety
- signs of shock (see also page 51).

You should immediately call an ambulance, giving as much detail as possible on the likely cause of the allergic reaction and symptoms. If the casualty has any medication for the allergy, ask them to take it, or help them administer it if necessary. Then treat as follows:

Conscious casualty

- Help them sit up in a position that eases their breathing, usually leaning forwards slightly.

Unconscious casualty

- If the casualty becomes unconscious and is not breathing sufficiently normally, follow the DRAB/C procedure (see pages 36–7)
- If they are unconscious but breathing as normally as possible in the circumstances, place in the recovery position (see page 38) until the ambulance arrives.

Asthma

Asthma is on the increase in young people, experts citing urban living and other lifestyle factors as a possible cause. The chances are that you will have one person, if not more, in your club with the condition. Air passages in the lungs spasm and linings of the airways swell, narrowing them and making breathing difficult. Likely triggers when you are supervising young people will be exercise, an allergic reaction (e.g. hay fever), a cold, or reaction to extremes of weather (e.g. a very cold or very hot day).

The chances are that anyone having an asthma attack will recognise their own symptoms, and will probably be able to deal with them in an assured manner. Usually, those who experience regular attacks carry a blue reliever (Ventolin) inhaler, which they can use unassisted, and maybe a spacer (plastic bottle-style attachment that acts to deliver the metered dose of inhalant more effectively). However, you should be aware of the symptoms should you have to step in and assist:

- The casualty will be having difficulty breathing, with a particularly long outward breath, which may also be wheezing
- A cough
- Hypoxia – a lack of oxygen in the blood – which may produce grey/blue tinge to the lips, ears and fingernail-beds caused by the deoxygenated haemoglobin.

However, younger children may need help with using their inhaler, or may be generally panicked or distressed. You should assist treatment as follows:

- Reassure the casualty and keep them calm
- Encourage them to use their inhaler/spacer, assisting if necessary
- Seat the casualty in a position where they can breathe the most easily – this is usually leaning forwards with arms resting on the table or the back of a chair – and encourage them to breathe slowly and deeply. Do not lay them down
- If the attack has not eased after three minutes, ask the casualty to use their inhaler again. If their condition deteriorates, seek medical assistance.

Note: If you are away from home and have young people with asthma in your care, ensure that they have sufficient inhaler medication with them for the time they are away, and that it is readily accessible should an attack occur (i.e. with the child on the coach and not stored in their luggage). For more on travelling with young people, see chapter 2, page 25.

Hypoglycaemia (low blood-sugar)

The chances are that you will only experience a casualty with hypoglycaemia if they are a diabetic, in which case they may, as with someone having an asthma attack, recognise the onset of a hypoglycaemic episode. It can also occur as a result of heat exhaustion (see page 52) or hypothermia (see page 55).

Symptoms to look out for are:

■ Deteriorating rate of response, and/or strange, confused or aggressive behaviour and actions
■ Weakness, faintness or hunger
■ Palpitations and muscle tremors
■ Sweaty and/or clammy, cold skin.

Conscious casualty

Your main objective for a conscious casualty is to raise blood-sugar levels as fast as possible to prevent further deterioration and unconsciousness:

■ Help the casualty to sit or lie down
■ If they are a diabetic with their own glucose gel, help them administer it
■ In the absence of glucose gel, give them a sugary drink (make sure they are not 'Diet' or 'Light' fizzy drinks as these are sugar-free), chocolate or any other sweet food to hand. You should only do this if the casualty is *fully conscious* and able to swallow food or drink without choking.
■ If the casualty recovers quickly, ask them to eat more food/drink, take some rest. Advise their parents to take them to the doctor
■ If the casualty shows little or no improvement, monitor their vital signs to assess other possible causes, and to ensure that they do not fall unconscious.

Unconscious casualty

■ If the casualty becomes unconscious and is not breathing sufficiently normally, follow the DRAB/C procedure (see pages 36–7)
■ If they are unconscious but breathing as normally as possible in the circumstances, place in the recovery position (see page 38) and call an ambulance.

Note: If you are away from home and have young people with diabetes in your care, ensure that they have sufficient insulin medication with them for the time they are away, and that it is readily accessible should hypoglycaemia occur. For more on travelling with young people, see chapter 2, page 25.

Foreign objects in the eye

On dusty playing surfaces, it is easy for a piece of grit or dust particles to fly up and get caught in the eye. It is also possible for other objects, such as contact lenses (more likely in the older members of your club) or an eyelash to cause discomfort.

Symptoms of a foreign object could be:

- eye redness and eye-watering
- pain and discomfort
- blurred vision
- involuntary blinking, eyelids screwed up in spasm.

You need to establish that an object is present and try to flush it out before it damages the eye:

- Seat the casualty somewhere in the light where you can see the eye clearly
- Separate the eyelids gently with the thumb or finger
- Ask the casualty to look up, down, left and right to see if you can see the object causing the problem.

If you can see the foreign object on the white of the eye:

- Tilt the head back and to the same side as the affected eye, and place a towel on the shoulder
- Wash the eye with clean water from a glass or, if available, sterile eyewash from an eye bath, pouring the water/eyewash from the bridge of the nose down through the eye towards the shoulder
- If this fails to flush the object, attempt to use a moist swab or the dampened corner of a tissue to pick up the loose object.

If none of the above works, or the object cannot be located, seek medical attention. If the object is on the iris (i.e. coloured part of the eye), do not attempt to remove it, as this may damage the eye. Instead, cover the eye with a patch and arrange for medical treatment at A&E.

A final word on the subject

If you are in any doubt about anything to do with the medical condition of someone, never feel afraid or embarrassed to call 999 and ask for emergency service help. It is better to have expert help quickly on the scene than you trying to be a hero or to have made a false alarm than failed to save a life for the sake of a phone call.

Just remember DRAB/C.

part 2
COACHING AND PLAYER DEVELOPMENT

chapter 4
COACHING

The role and impact of the coach

Ask any top footballer to name the most important influence on their career and they are likely to refer to a coach, either past or present. Many footballers would not be where they are today without the help, influence and guidance of one or more coaches. Whether playing football at the highest professional level or simply for fun, the importance of a good coach cannot be underestimated. The FA, through its extensive training programme for coaches, has always made it a priority to improve the technical quality of coaching. This reaps rewards on pitches up and down the country.

We must remember that coaches, just like teachers, help shape the thoughts, actions, behaviour, respect levels and discipline of those they tutor, particularly youngsters. Coaches have to be aware that the way they react, what they say and how they approach issues and reach decisions can be mimicked by those in their care.

So the message here is to follow the coaches' code of conduct (*see* Chapter 1). Encourage your pupils to adopt the codes of conduct for players. Ask parents to help you manage the coaching of their child in a positive and dynamic way. Remember, you cannot please everyone all the time, and there will be occasions when a child or youth becomes impossible to control or teach through no fault of yours. A disruptive element needs to be dealt with in a positive yet firm manner. The backing of a strong committee should ensure that coaches follow good codes of practice, and that parents and players do likewise.

Formulas for good coaching
Coaches' checklist

Before any training session or match, coaches should ensure all the following procedures are in place.
- Structured warm-up and warm-down
- Stretcher and first aid kit available

- First-aider on site
- Written first aid procedures available
- Telephone available with list of emergency and contact numbers
- Players are wearing shin pads
- Plenty of drinks available
- Players have removed all jewellery
- Players are fit for the activity
- Players know the name and location of the venue in case they need to call the emergency services

Coaching points

- Use guided discovery – ask players if they can see or try another way to improve something
- Demonstrate
- Make your point quickly and concisely
- Give plenty of praise
- Use the formula: Stop, Question, Demo, Rehearse, Play

Coaching qualifications

Becoming a coach

The first step to becoming a coach is to enrol on an FA coaching course (contact your local FA for details – visit www.thefa.com). Getting on the coaching ladder gives you the opportunity to progress through the various FA coaching qualifications and to enhance your skills and knowledge. Experience is essential for a coach as so much can be learned from the coaching field, whether it is working with other coaches and learning from them or coaching different groups of players with mixed abilities. A successful coach should always be open to new ideas and want to improve their individual skills and knowledge of the game.

The FA Coaches Association (FACA)

The FA Coaches Association offers you the opportunity to be part of the professional body of like-minded coaches interested in the development of individuals. Members are required to abide by a code of conduct (see Chapter 1). Every coach who is a full member of FACA is provided with comprehensive insurance.

For more information visit http://www.thefa.com/TheFA/FALearning/FACA

Developing good habits, early

Discipline

A child brought up to respect the property of others, to be polite, kind, thoughtful and considerate will tend to continue this attitude and approach as they grow up. On the whole, if we can teach children good habits early, we will see them use these social skills throughout their lives.

Football players have to socialise, work as a team, give up certain personal agendas and share in group successes and disappointments. All these elements are 'character building' and help shape the emotional and mental behaviour of an individual, hopefully in a balanced way.

As coaches and guardians of children at our clubs, we constantly need to remind players of their responsibility for their actions, habits and behaviour. How they manage these will determine how socially acceptable they are and how emotionally and mentally balanced they will be throughout life. Naturally, coaches need to be vigilant and help players to recognise ways to handle situations that will benefit them in the future, but without imposing their way as right or the only way.

Here are some hints that coaches may wish to take on board when dealing with their students:

- Communication is the first step to success for every coach.
- Be clear in your messages – do not allow opportunity for misinterpretation.
- Be proactive – do not hope a problem you see will just go away.
- Use positive language – challenge players to improve rather than punish them.
- Never assume.
- Make all communication seem important.
- Show respect to all players.
- Allow time for everybody.
- Never promise anything you cannot deliver.
- Balance praise with constructive criticism.
- Focus on the correction, not the mistake.
- Learn to be a good listener.
- Learn to be a good questioner.
- Be aware of cultural differences.
- Use players' names and know something of their families and lifestyle.
- Be prepared – start with the end in mind.
- Criticise only performance, not the person.
- Avoid communication when out of control emotionally.

- Make maximum use of informal meeting opportunities.
- Use fun – humour is a great stress reliever.
- Always end communications by clarifying what you have agreed upon.
- Always use the word 'we'.
- Use the 'guided discovery' coaching method whenever possible, which focuses on asking the player to think and say if there is something they could do to improve things. The player, not the coach, solves a problem.

Influential and respected sports psychologists appear to agree that behaviour = personality × environment. So, as a coach it is important that you get the best from your players by adapting your coaching to the individual learning needs of your players in a positive and encouraging way. Make it fun.

chapter 5

WARMING UP

The warm-up before the start of a football match or training session takes only a few minutes. A proper warm-up prepares the body for exercise, warms the muscles, and enables the body to cope better with the strains of knocks and sudden movements that cause injuries. Warming up can prevent serious injury, and the stretching exercises promote agility. If players pull a hamstring or get a back injury, they can be out of soccer for months, and such injuries are often avoidable.

Before you start the warm-up, make sure players are aware of the following essential guidelines:

- Make movements smooth, not jerky.
- Do not over-stretch.
- Slight pain is normal; they should feel the muscle stretch.
- They should not feel any severe or stabbing pains; if they do, they must stop immediately.
- Breathe normally during these exercises.
- Repeat each stretch several times and hold for 5–10 seconds.

The three-phase warm-up

The following football warm-up gradually increases in intensity and follows a logical pattern. You can substitute different activities to form your own workouts, being mindful of the objectives set for each phase.

This warm-up involves three separate phases of work. In each, the intensity of effort is increased from the previous level, giving a gradual progression towards the fully prepared state.

For each phase of the warm-up there are:

- Objectives
- Suggested activities
- Heart rate ranges to achieve objectives

This warm-up lasts for 20 minutes. Each phase may be reduced if you have less time. You should also tailor the warm-up to the age of the players involved. Younger players, say 10–12 year olds, may require a shorter, less intense warm-up, perhaps just 10 minutes and with more emphasis on fun. It is also important to remember that children lose heat more easily than adults so may require additional clothing to maintain body temperature. For older players, it is important that they are taught good habits regarding the phases of warm-up and the correct methods of stretching. Coaches should not let senior/adult players simply go through the motions of a warm-up – it is a recipe for an early injury.

Phase 1
Objectives
- Gradually raise pulse rate from resting levels
- Preparatory stretching

Content
- Slow jogging, stop, turn, at a low intensity, skipping, backwards and sideways jogging

Duration: 5 minutes

Heart rate target for players: 120–140 beats per minute

- Preparatory stretches: calves, hamstrings, quads, hip flexors, lower back – all stretches to be held for only 5 seconds

Duration: 1 minute 30 seconds

Phase 2
Objectives
- Further increase heart rate through higher-intensity activities involving changes of direction and greater distances to cover
- Begin some longer-hold stretching on major muscle groups

Content
- Faster jogging followed by striding out, slight changes of direction, high knees, heel flicks

Duration: 5 minutes

Heart rate target for players: 120–160 beats per minute

- Stretches for: calves, hamstrings, quads, adductors, hip flexors, lower back and gluteals – all stretches to be held for 10 seconds

Duration: 2 minutes 30 seconds

Phase 3
Objectives

- Increase heart rate to final working level
- Full-hold stretches
- Specific movements used in the game

Content

- Striding out followed by sprinting over varying distances, specific movements e.g. jump and head, turn and sprint, repeated sprint work of short duration, backing off, jockeying

Duration: 5 minutes

Heart rate target for players: 160–200 beats per minute

- Stretches for: calves, hamstrings, quads, hips, adductors and gluteals – all stretches to be held for 10–15 seconds

Duration: 3 minutes

Following this warm-up, players should return to some high-intensity sprinting and specific movements such as jumping, heading, turning and sprinting, jockeying to ensure full readiness for the game.

Warm-up for under 10s

Stretching exercises are not necessary for this age group, and the warm-up need only be brief. Some jogging, swinging of the arms, twists of the hips or other movements to loosen up will suffice. It is, however, important to do some warm-up and cool-down routines – albeit short in duration and concentration – to build discipline in youngsters for later life.

Warm-up for 10–12-year-olds

A 10-minute warm-up is all that is necessary, and over-stretching at this age can even be harmful. Perform the first phase of the adult warm-up (*see* above) consisting of jogging followed by one round of *gentle* stretching with five-second holds. Follow this with a few minutes practising ball control skills – passing and movement exercises are particularly good.

Warm-up for 13-year-olds and over

Start your soccer warm-up with some gentle exercise, such as jogging. The aim is to raise the heart rate to around 120 beats per minute. Then perform some *gentle* stretches, holding for about five seconds on each stretch. Work with a ball in a team game of some kind that blends exercise and stretches, gently increasing heart rate. A particular favourite of mine involves teams of four, split into two players (numbered one and three) opposite the other two (numbered two and four), 10 metres apart. Player one passes the ball to player two and follows the pass to join the back of the queue. Simply rotate all the players. Different drills can be completed, such as simple passes, chipped passes and running with the ball. You could pop a cone or two down in the middle as an obstacle for players to go around. Another idea for four players is to get one player to stand in each corner of a 10-metre square. Player one passes the ball to an available player and follows the pass in to take their place. This enjoyable, high-tempo exercise includes all the elements necessary to prepare players for the game ahead.

Pre-match warm-up drills

Here are some more fun warm-up activities. They can all be carried out within an area of 10 m × 20 m or 10 m × 30 m, depending on the age group. Remember to stop after every two or three minutes for players to stretch muscle groups or have a drink.

Throw and catch
Get the players to jog within the whole area, throwing and catching a ball (a bit like rugby passing). Use three or four footballs in the grid.

- For very young kids, work within a smaller 10 m × 20 m area. Also, remember that young players may not be able to catch or are perhaps a little frightened of the ball, so let them hand the ball to a teammate and run off to find someone else to take a ball from. Alternatively, they could pass the ball with a foot.
- Progress this activity for older players, so that the throw is for a header or a volley, or a thigh control and volley, etc. Each time, the thrower gives the ball back to the partner so that everyone gets to head, volley and so on.
- To ensure players get maximum benefit from these exercises, encourage them to move into another 10 m × 10 m grid rather than stay in the same area.

Sprinting and jogging

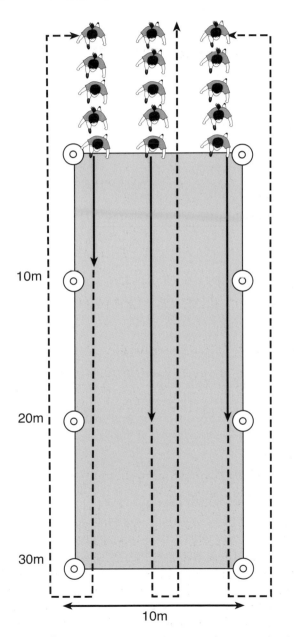

This is designed for older kids and adults (11-a-side). Place cones at 10-metre intervals over 30 metres in length. Split the team into three groups of five in lines at one end of the grid. You can use a mixture of short sprints, jogs and dynamic stretches over 10 and 20 metres. The final 10 and 20 metres should be used for recovery – either walking or light jogging.

Here are some suggestions for four exercises:

- A short sprint – do this twice.
- Sideways crab sprints – do this twice.
- Sweep-the-floor type run – do this twice.
- A high knee sprint – do this twice.

Ensure players do the full recovery jog through to the end and back down to join the queue. Note the direction so that players don't bump into each other. Do the four exercise repetitions and then allow players to have a minute of static stretching and a drink. One final note: let a player cover 10 metres before the next player goes.

Here are a few ideas for other exercises that the players can do.

- Sprint 10 m – jog
- Turn left knee 'out' 10 m – jog
- Turn right knee 'out' 10 m – jog
- As above, only turn knee 'in' 10 m – jog
- High knees 20 m – jog
- Swivel hips right and left (swing arms in sync with hip rotations) 20 m – jog
- Side steps right – three strides – then left then back to right and so on – forwards 20 m – jog
- Side steps right – three strides – then left then back to right and so on – backwards 20 m – jog
- Heels (bring heels up to bottom) 20 m – jog
- Sprint 20 m – jog

To turn the knee 'in' or 'out', players bring their knee up vertically as they jog forwards and turn it in (across them) or out.

Passing in zones
Younger children

For children under 10 in mini soccer, use the 10 m × 20 m grid split into two equal zones. You can work with the ball in an enjoyable way that will also tune players into the game.

Split the team: in each zone put three against one (one in a bib) or four against one, depending on numbers. The idea is for the three or four players in zone one to pass the ball around within the zone while the bibbed player tries to intercept the ball. After two or three passes, a player in zone one passes the ball into zone two where the game continues in the same way. After one minute, change the bibbed player.

NOTE: for the very young, the coach should be the bibbed player and cannot tackle or intercept.

The coach should help the players by making it obvious, with their position and angle, which is the best pass for the player with the ball to make. The coach can easily cover both zones and should not insist that young players pass any set number of times before sending the ball into the other zone.

Older children

Children over 11 years up to adult should use the 10 m × 30 m grid divided into three zones. Split the team: put five in zone one and the same in zone two. Four extra players in bibs 'pair-up' – one pair will operate in zone one and the other in zone two. When one pair is not working to intercept the ball in a zone they should 'recover' in the recovery zone.

The idea is for the players in zone one to pass the ball around within the zone while the bibbed players try to intercept it. After three or four passes, a player in zone one passes or chips the ball into zone two where the game continues in the same way. The players in the recovery zone cannot intercept at this stage. If the bibbed players succeed in intercepting the ball, get them to swap with other players. If they do not succeed, change the bibbed players after two minutes.

The coach can progress this exercise by asking the bibbed players in the recovery zone to try and intercept the pass from one zone to another. This encourages non-bibbed players on both sides to see an opportunity to pass, and the receiving players to move to accept a good 'safe' pass. Further progression can include lifting the restriction on the number of passes in a zone before transfer of the ball. This encourages the players to see and react to forward passing opportunities.

Whatever the age group of the players, this drill acts as a great match warm-up or training session drill. Every player is involved and can learn many things: how to receive a ball, when to pass, where to pass, who to 'shut down', communication, awareness of others and much more besides. Remember to change the bibbed players often and offer drinks as appropriate.

Mini-match

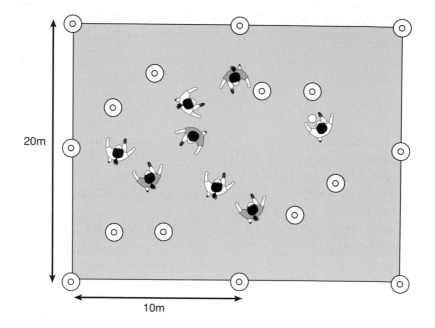

This is another 'closing' warm-up drill that kids and adults love. Use a 20 m × 20 m grid. Split the team in half with one side wearing a distinctive coloured bib. The aim is to win a point or goal simply by passing the ball through one of the gates – marked by two space markers or poles – to a teammate. The coach – on the outside – needs to have a ball with them always to keep play moving. This encourages passing, tackling, defending, switching play and many other key elements of the game while generating a lot of fun and friendly 'competition'.

Conclusion

In a small area, a coach can conduct a warm-up session that involves all the elements of running, stretching, teamwork, concentration/focus and ball play in a highly effective way. All the exercises should include regular breaks for static stretching or taking a drink on board.

For children under 10, the whole warm-up period should be around 15 minutes. Children aged 11–14 can warm up for up to 30 minutes, while anything up to 40 minutes can be allowed for adults.

chapter 6
COACHING THE BASIC SKILLS

This chapter is designed to help coaches get the right techniques across to players. Teaching good techniques in the basic soccer skills, especially to the very young, is of paramount importance if they are to be good footballers in the future. Good coaches are not there to try and coach flair and panache but to help players improve their technique and become confident in using their natural abilities.

Players should have fun while learning these skills. Don't scold a player for not getting the technique right. Instead, praise them for their efforts. Taking time to teach basic skills will bring many rewards for coaches as they slowly start to see the young players in their care blossom.

Kicking the ball

Soccer kicking techniques range from basic shooting and passing skills to advanced techniques, such as bending the ball around a wall and penalty kicks. It is important to start with the basics – ensure that players master the key skills using the instep and inside of the foot. Over 50 per cent of youth players use incorrect technique, which results in inaccurate passes that do not have the right pace or stay on the ground.

The instep

The instep, the part of the foot where the laces are, provides both power and control – it is used for the majority of kicking in a game. The most common mistake made by beginners is to use the toe. Not only is this painful if somebody tackles hard when they are trying to kick, but it can also be very inaccurate. The advantage of the instep is that it presents a flat surface to the ball, and can also be used to make the ball swerve, curve and dip.

The non-kicking leg provides support, and should be bent as players kick. When we want to keep the ball on the ground, the head is down, over the ball. The follow-through should be long and smooth, and another useful tip is to approach the kick slightly from the side.

The lofted kick

The lofted kick is used to play the long ball, cross the ball into the penalty area, and to clear the ball from defence. It is the only technique for lifting the ball into the air with real power.

A goalkeeper with good kicking technique can create an attacking situation with good length and accuracy of a kick. Goalkeepers should regularly practise this type of kick as goal kicks are a regular occurrence in matches.

Coaching tips

- To achieve height, players should lean back as they strike the ball.
- To bend the ball, players should kick the ball below the mid-line and slightly to one side.
- To keep balance, players should place the non-kicking foot slightly in front of the ball instead of level with it, and put their arms out.
- It is important to obtain distance from the kick as well as height – the object is to kick the ball high enough to clear any opposition players, but extra height is not necessary and will reduce the length of the kick.

Corners

The lofted kick is generally used for taking corners, preferably with some spin applied to swerve the ball (*see* below). Corners are excellent goal scoring opportunities because the ball can be crossed directly into the most dangerous area of the pitch, in front of goal. A well-directed header from a corner kick is generally all that is needed to score a goal. Corners should be practised and involve players moving into target areas – namely near post, penalty spot and far post (*see* 'Crosses', below).

It is worth working on strategy for corner kicks in your team's coaching sessions. All too often I watch teams who only ever kick the ball into a crowded goalmouth. Apart from being predictable, it can only have a 50 per cent chance of success, and with a goalkeeper able to jump and catch the ball the odds are probably less.

Coaching tips

- Do you want corners to swing in towards goal or out away from goal? This will require a corner on the right to be taken by a player using their left foot or right foot respectively.

- Work on passing the ball firmly into a player at the near post who can direct the ball away from goal for a shot by an incoming teammate.

- Play the short corner to a full back who has timed their run late to catch the opposition by surprise.

- By varying your corners, you can create many more goal scoring opportunities.

Crosses

There are three main types of cross:

1. The near post cross
2. The cross to the penalty spot
3. The far post cross

At **the near post** the attacker tries to get in front of the defender, ideally with a run towards goal to obtain momentum. Depending on the type of pass made, the player at the near post can get a 'flick-on' to divert the ball crossed in or control the ball with a returned pass. Often the kicking technique here is a short 'chip' into the near post or perhaps a low-driven strike/pass into the feet of the near post runner.

The **cross to the penalty spot** should be met by a player powerfully and confidently running into the box from the edge of the 18-yard area. A coaching tip here is to practise 'timing' of the run and to be aware of the curve on the ball. For instance, a right-footed cross from the right wing will often curve away from the goal. Therefore it is more successful if the run is late to meet the ball rather than early, risking getting under the ball or the ball curving behind you.

At the far post the attacker usually tries to get behind the defence, on the blind side. This type of cross tends to favour taller player who can jump high over the defence, whereas shorter players are better placed at the near post.

Both corner kicks and general crossing of the ball should be regularly brought into coaching sessions for all age groups. Strategically, these can be potent weapons in the team's armoury, so practising different moves is well worth it. My advice for coaching corners and crosses is to mix it up. Try short and long crosses. Try angled back passes and chain passes across the pitch. Coach good tactical movement in the goal area, and so on. Have a few 'set' routines and get your corner-taker to signify which technique or type of cross they intend to make.

Chipping

The chip is a kicking technique used to lift the ball quickly over short distances. The disadvantage of the chip over the lofted kicking technique is that it lacks power. The advantages are that lift can be produced quickly, and that the backspin generated from this method causes the ball to slow down on hitting the ground.

The chip uses a stabbing or chopping motion in which the lower part of the foot, but not the toe, makes contact low down on the ball. The knee of the kicking foot is bent, and high at the end of the follow-through. As for the lofted kick, it is best to lean back slightly, but with the head looking down at the ball. A useful tip is to place the non-kicking foot slightly behind the ball.

Learning how to take a cross in football requires mastering several different skills:
- The kicking technique needs to be correct.
- The player must have vision and awareness of whom to aim the cross for.
- The player must be able to create space for the cross under pressure from defenders.

The kicking technique for crossing the ball is to use the instep, getting underneath the ball, and preferably to put some spin on the ball to bend it away from the goalkeeper or to put curl on the ball to keep it in play. This makes the cross harder to intercept. Sometimes, a player will find themselves having to cross the ball from a very square position close to the touchline. In this case it might be necessary to use the area around the big toe for kicking the ball in order to keep it in play.

Corner and crossing drills

For the very young – up to eight or nine years of age – use a light or soft ball to throw into an area for a header or shot at goal. Start by having no goalkeeper so that the youngsters enjoy the experience of scoring. Put the players in groups of three and work on their movement to meet the ball being thrown in and the correct techniques for heading (downwards) and striking the ball (keeping it low enough to hit the target). Also work on the timing of their runs to 'meet' the ball, rather than getting too far forward so the ball goes over their heads. Mix up the throws to the near and far posts as well as the penalty spot area. Gradually introduce a goalkeeper as the players become more confident and able.

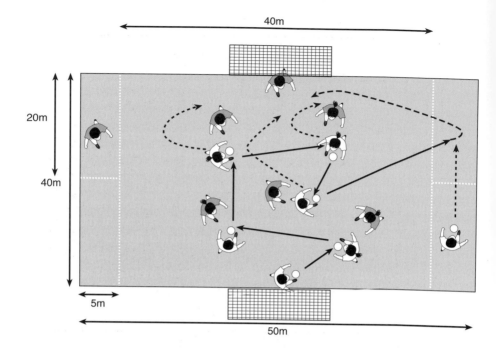

Another drill is to position cones down the line of the 18-yard area on both sides of the field and about another 5–10 metres or so in. This will create a channel for a wide player to run into before crossing. Line your defenders and attackers up about 30 metres out from the defending goal. Start the drill with midfield players in the centre circle passing the ball around. After three or four passes, play the ball into one of the channels for a winger or full back to run on to. Their job is to run the ball through the channel and whip a cross in. The attackers must support the play and get on the end of the cross while midfield players support them for any short clearances. Defenders will have to retreat and defend the cross while the goalkeeper is forced to decide whether to come and collect the cross or stay and defend the goal. Practise this from both right and left wings.

A drill for older players – 12-year-olds and above – is the highly intensive and fast-paced 'crossing rotation drill'. This must be high tempo but with regular breaks for recovery and drinks. Work in a 60 m × 40 m area with a channel down each side. Split the outfield players into two sides with distinctive coloured bibs and position in the centre of the pitch, with two players on each side in the channel, as shown. Goalkeepers start the drill with a throw to one of their teammates in the channel (in the full back position). The ball is passed into the feet of one of the attacking group who comes short for the pass and then lays it out into the channel for the winger to run on to and cross. Three attacking players make runs to meet the cross with a header or shot. The other side now become the attackers and the process begins again on the other side of the pitch.

Once you have worked on crosses from the right (clockwise), progress the drill to work from the left (anticlockwise). A further progression is for the player receiving the ball from the goalkeeper to act as a defender on the opposite cross or for two players of the opposition to act as defenders, tracking the runs of the attackers. This offers overload for the attackers and improves decision making of the runs and crosses.

Free kicks

Taking free kicks is an important skill that requires awareness of football tactics as well as sound technique. Free kicks provide an opportunity to control play, and around the penalty area they are goal scoring opportunities. The coach should plan several attacking set plays with his team, including free kicks from different angles, so that each player knows what they should be doing.

When taking free kicks around the penalty area, the fewer touches before shooting at goal the better. Teams and coaches should aim for a direct shot or a single pass before shooting, because set plays involving more than one pass allow plenty of time for the defence to organise and close down.

In training, work on a variety of set plays such as:

- A direct shot around or over the wall
- A pass to the side of the wall followed by a shot at goal
- A chip over the wall towards the edge of the six-yard box, aiming for a player to head into goal or control and shoot

In the midfield, free kicks are opportunities to build an attack. Look to take the free kick quickly if there is a player with space, but otherwise allow time for your own team to push forward.

In defence, free kicks are similar to goal kicks with the choice of playing a short or a long ball. This will depend on your team's strengths and tactics, but the ball should always be cleared from dangerous positions. This usually means long, high and wide kicks.

Bending the ball

Bending or swerving the ball is one of the most exciting soccer kicking techniques. Brazilians, such as Pelé, were famous for making the ball bend around a defensive wall, and this is one of the hallmarks of David Beckham. This skill is important in many areas of football, such as shots at goal around defenders who are obscuring the goalkeeper's view, corner kicks, crosses into the box, and passing the ball around opponents.

There are two main methods: using the outside of the foot to swerve the ball away from you, or using the inside of the foot to bend the ball inwards. Swerve is produced by kicking the ball off-centre on the opposite side to the side you want the ball to swerve to. For example, if a player wants to bend the ball from right to left with their right foot, they should make contact with the ball on the right side using the inside of the foot. To make the ball bend away from them from left to right, they should kick the ball on the left side using the outside of the foot.

Volleying

Volley technique is a difficult soccer skill to master, but volleys have produced many spectacular goals. Volleying requires the player to strike through the ball, keeping the knee level or over the ball rather than under it, which has the effect of keeping the ball on a straight trajectory.

As well as goal scoring, volleys can be used for passing, and kicking the ball away from danger. In tight situations, it is often better for a defender to volley the ball away than try to control it at a difficult height.

Keeping the ball down is one of the important aspects of volleying technique. As with all kicking skills, watching the ball and keeping the head down helps, but it is important to try to keep the knee over the ball.

Coaching tips

One of the secrets of great volleys is the swivel motion.

- The player starts from a square position with both feet a comfortable distance apart.
- Then, without moving their feet, the player twists the upper body to the right until the left shoulder is facing directly in front.
- Next, the player twists back until the right shoulder is facing in front.
- This can be practised without a ball.
- For a left-footed volley, twist first to the left and then to the right.

Passing the ball

Passing techniques are vital for keeping possession and controlling the game, and many parts of the foot can be used. Technically, any ball that reaches a player on the same team is a pass – be it a kick, header or even a throw-in – so nearly all the sections in this chapter relate to passing (and controlling and receiving the ball, *see* below, which are equally important). However, there are a couple of specific points that should be made.

Inside of the foot 'push' pass

The simplest and best technique for short passes is with the head over the ball, the body well balanced, and the ball kicked with the inside of the foot, which is the flattest part of the foot. This is known as the 'push' pass. Sometimes this technique is used for short-range shots at goal, and even for taking penalties, because of its reliability. The disadvantage is the lack of power. Accurate short passes with supporting runs into space allow a team to keep possession and build an attack.

Coaching the 'push' pass

- Get the player to face the target so the ball and target are in a straight line.
- Place the 'plant' foot alongside the ball, with toes pointing towards the target.
- The head should be over the ball, looking down, and both knees slightly bent.
- Teach the proper motion by first having the player place their striking foot flat against the back of the ball, pushing the ball towards the target and following through.
- Now ask them to do the same, but this time taking one step into the ball. This step provides power to the pass. If the pass goes into the air it means it was struck below the mid-line of the ball.

Passing drills

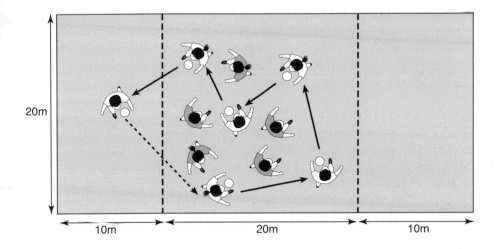

There are many soccer drills for passing skills, and one of the most enjoyable is a five-a-side game played within a 40 m × 20 m area. Zone off two 'end zones', 20 m × 10 m as shown. Quite simply, play five against five in the middle zone, and a goal is scored when a pass is made from a player in the middle to a teammate running into an end zone. Football is a 360-degree game so players should be allowed to score with a pass into either end zone. Restart each time with a feed from the side into the middle zone. This drill encourages players to create and move into space to receive a pass, and others to move to open up opportunities to score a goal or point.

5m

Here's a passing drill for young players. Pair up players opposite each other. One passes to the other, who controls the ball and passes it back to their partner. Get the players to move out to 20 metres apart. As the passes are being made and on the call of the coach, get one side to gradually come in, five metres at a time, until the players are passing just five metres.

This drill has several skill components within it: the cushion control, pace and accuracy of the passing and receiving. Getting the players to move in closer and then further away helps them grasp the art of 'weighting' the ball with greater or lesser power. Remember to add communication in the drill and get the players to praise their partner if they do something well.

A progression for the drill is to get players on either side to swap with the player to their right or left each time they pass the ball. This adds receiving the ball on the move, is a great warm-up exercise and brings some lively fun and enjoyment to the drill, especially when the players are only five metres apart.

Heading the ball

Heading techniques are vital in the game of football. The team that dominates in the air can win the ball in the danger zone in front of the six-yard box when both defending and attacking, and can win the ball from long goal kicks. Heading skills also enable a team to use the long ball tactic effectively for flick-ons and nod-downs. This can very quickly turn a defensive situation into a goal scoring one.

Coaching tips

The correct part of the head to use is the forehead. This is the hardest and flattest part of the head, and with the eyes open on contact will give better control and greater power.

You often see youngsters playing football who can play the ball well on the ground, but are not confident when the ball is played in the air. Often the problem is a fear of getting hurt, but once they learn to head the ball properly using the forehead, there is no danger.

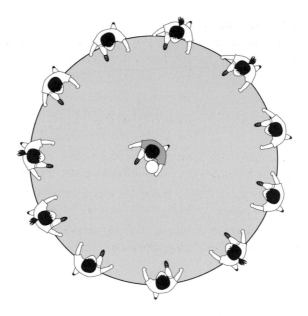

A useful way to introduce under-eights to heading is to play some fun games. One I particularly like is the head-catch game with a soft, spongy ball or an indoor soft football (looks like a big tennis ball). Arrange your players in a circle not too far away from you and close enough for a gentle throw of the ball to reach them.

The coach stands in the middle with the ball and moves around the circle. As the ball travels to a player, the coach calls out if it is to be caught or headed. The coach can mix things up by going in different directions and choosing players at random. To progress this game, the coach can ask the players to do the opposite things to the call – so a catch becomes a header and vice versa.

Defensive heading

Defensive heading techniques enable a player to direct the ball upwards in such situations as clearing the ball from defence. Any qualified coach will tell you that the key ingredients to a good defensive header are 'high, long and wide'.

Coaching tip

- The key to the defensive header is to start with the forehead underneath the ball, so that the head can move upwards to attack the ball.
- The player's eyes must remain below the ball, so that at the moment the forehead makes contact with the ball, the head is moving upwards.
- The player should use their legs to push upwards just before heading the ball as this helps to obtain good distance.

A useful and fun game for beginners and more experienced players is heading the football over a volleyball net. Since the ball has to be directed upwards to clear the net, it is particularly good practice for defensive heading. It is also a great way for players to learn control and direction.

Attacking heading

Attacking heading techniques are used for directing the ball downwards to score goals and win the ball in the air. The key to the attacking header is to get the eyes focused on the ball and to get the forehead over the ball, thus attacking the ball from above.

Beginners often have trouble timing the header, and end up hitting the nose or the top of the head, so coaches should start young children with a soft ball. It is important to teach players to watch the ball carefully. Balance is another point to watch – try to encourage beginners to get their feet into position early so that they are behind the ball. A useful drill to help young players learn the technique of a downward attacking header is to use a target on the ground – something like a cone or circle of space-markers a few feet away. Pair up players opposite each other and have a competition to see who can be the first to hit the target five times.

More able and older players should work on meeting crosses on the move, so that their momentum helps add power to the header, and to avoid being caught static by defenders. Players should aim to head the ball downwards into areas where goalkeepers find it most difficult to get down.

A good drill for this is to start with a line of players on the edge of the 18-yard area where it meets the 'D'. The coach stands on the corner of the six-yard area where it meets the base line to the penalty spot area and throws a ball towards the penalty spot for a player to run in and meet the ball with an attacking header. Put a goalkeeper in goal to help the attacking players head the ball wide of the goalkeeper but inside the posts. The coach can move up the six-yard line to vary the angles of delivery. As players become more expert, crosses can be delivered from wide areas for attackers to meet the ball. The next progression is to introduce a defender or two.

Several factors help players obtain power when attacking a header. The shoulders can be pushed forwards and the back arched before attacking the ball. The upper body should be kept in a straight line, not falling away to the side, and much of the power comes from the neck muscles. It is very important to be positive and always to focus on the ball.

Diving headers

The diving header technique gives a footballer that extra edge and versatility to reach the ball first and to get a head on crosses that would otherwise be missed. This is particularly true at the near post where the attacker is trying to get in front of the defender.

The diving header requires getting both feet off the ground, and a jump towards the football. The player should be almost horizontal as they head the ball, using their forehead (as always). Generally, takeoff is from only one foot because the diving header is usually attempted on the run. Players must keep their eyes open as this will help to direct the header goalwards.

Most players find the dive the most difficult part of this technique. Players who are having problems should practise without the ball. Put a low hurdle down, such as a large bag, a couple of twigs, or even a player crouched down if you can find a volunteer! Get the player to jump the hurdle without hesitating. Then try the same thing with someone serving the ball so that the player jumps over the hurdle to head the ball.

Dribbling skills

Dribbling is all about close control and confidence. Improving close control and dribbling skills in football is vital for a player to be able to create space, keep possession and beat defenders. Close control is essential for every player on the field, including the goalkeeper. It generally refers to running with the ball and dribbling skills, but it can also include the first touch, and control with the foot, thigh, chest and head. Close control is a vital part of football coaching.

Running with the ball

Running with the ball is the first stage of close control. The aim is to keep the ball within your control without needing to break your stride. This technique uses the instep or, more commonly, the outside of the foot, which gives greater fluency of movement and ball control. On the field of play, running with the ball often occurs when a wide player has got past a defender and has 20 or 30 metres of clear space in front of them. They need to cover the ground quickly and still be in a position to deliver a cross for the attacking teammates. Improving close control also requires turning ability (*see* below).

Coaches should encourage players to begin dribbling at slow speeds, and then gradually build up speed. A simple exercise to help learn running with the ball is to build an obstacle course with cones or other markers placed at varying distances apart, and at different angles to each other. The object is to run with the ball as quickly as possible from cone to cone, but coming to a complete stop at each cone. This teaches close control, running, accelerating and stopping with the ball.

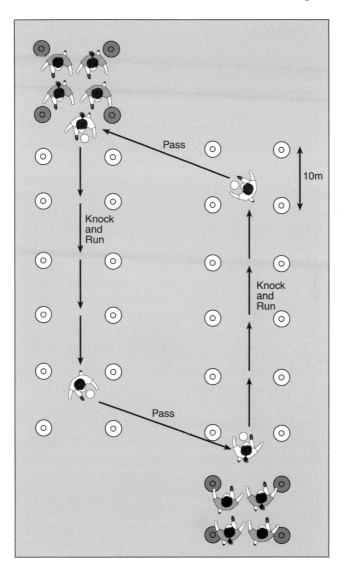

Another popular drill is to place two corridors of space-markers in a straight line 10 metres apart and up to 40 metres long. At each end of the corridor place four space-markers in a 10 m × 10 m square where the players wait. Split your players into two groups: one group at one end in a square; the other in the other square. The first player runs the ball through the corridor and at the end passes diagonally to a player waiting in the square who repeats the exercise. The key factors are a good first touch on receiving the ball out and in front of you into your path, to knock the ball no more than 10 metres at a time in a straight line and be able to make a good quality pass at the end of the run. Try to get players to use the instep or outside of the foot for greater control. Keep this going until all players have grasped the drill.

If you have enough players, set up another similar area and spilt the players into two teams. Each team player must have a minimum of four touches of the ball on the way out turn, and a minimum of four touches on the way back before passing to the next player. The winners are the team who go through the exercise, get back to their starting positions first and sit down or raise their hands.

The body swerve

The body swerve is a close control, dribbling skill used for running at and beating defenders, and creating space to shoot or pass the ball. The aim of the body swerve is to dummy the defender into moving the wrong way. In the game of soccer the body swerve is one of the most effective dribbling tricks, and was superbly demonstrated by the late Sir Stanley Matthews.

The body swerve builds upon basic turning skills (*see* below), and coaches should make sure that young players are able to turn with the ball under close control to the left and right.

Coaching tips

- With the ball on the right foot, the player should dip their left shoulder, and start to transfer body weight as if they are going to the left.

- However, instead of turning to the left, the player should quickly lean to the right, transferring weight to this side and using the left foot as a springboard to accelerate away to the right.

- The movement is reversed when using the left foot.

- Players should be encouraged to use both feet during drills, otherwise they will become predictable to defenders in the game.

- Speed is important – both acceleration and the ability to change speeds quickly.

Training drills for the body swerve include one-against-one exercises in front of goal. The object need not always be to go past the defender, but could be just to make space to shoot. The slalom is a good exercise for training when you are on your own, remembering to dip the shoulder.

Selling the dummy

There are many different types of dummy a player can use to confuse a defender. The objective is always to send an opponent the wrong way, take them by surprise or force them to make a tackle.

Defenders do not know what an attacker is going to do – they have to keep watch on the ball, be aware of their position and try to force attackers into 'safe' areas away from goal. Attacking players should be coached to remember that they have this upper hand and initiative over their opponents.

Leaving the ball

The simplest dummy is leaving the ball. This is an opportunistic move in which the ball is typically allowed to pass through the legs to another player who is in a better position.

The step-over

This trick often sends a defender one way, making it difficult for them to recover. It requires the attacker to transfer their body weight to one side, moving the foot towards the ball as if turning to that side, but at the last moment stepping over the ball, and keeping going in the same or opposite direction. A variation is to move the foot around the ball instead of over it, taking it in the opposite direction. Again, defenders will be sent one way, making it hard to shift direction and put a tackle in.

Stop-start

Another effective dummy is the stop-start move. The technique is to step on the ball with the sole of one foot, and then kick the ball forwards with the other foot. The aim is to do this as one movement without actually stopping. Defenders will often be forced to make a tackle and be caught off-balance.

Dummy drills

Each week set 10 minutes aside to get your players to practise a trick or dummy. For five- to seven-year-olds, place up to three space-markers in front of an empty goal 10 metres out. The space-markers can be placed in a variety of formations such as a zigzag, straight line or slalom. Each player runs the ball towards the space-markers and tries a trick to pass them and fire home a goal. This has a terrific outcome for the young players: they learn different types of dummy, they gain confidence and they score goals. Ask players to practise during the week and to show you the results at the next training session.

15m

For eight- to ten-year-olds you can introduce a goalkeeper in a mini-goal. Players still have to beat the space-markers with dummies and tricks but now have to decide whether to shoot or take on the goalkeeper.

For 11-year-olds and above, introduce a defender and consider attackers working from a static start in a straight line or perhaps a rolling passed ball from an angle. Mix it up to bring realism into the session.

Ball juggling

Football juggling skills and tricks are not just a means of showing off. They are excellent training methods for improving ball control, balance, first touch and general technique. Many coaches recommend starting a coaching session, whether for youth or adult players, with five minutes of ball juggling.

Juggling can be done using the top of the foot, the sides of the foot, the thigh or the head. There are also a number of tricks that involve throwing the ball up and catching it. The ball can be caught using the top of the foot, the thigh, the chest and even the back of the neck.

The goal with juggling is simple – players try to beat their personal best score of how many touches they can make without letting the ball fall to the floor. Beginners can start by juggling with the foot, and allowing the ball to bounce once between touches. They should progress quickly to not allowing the ball to bounce at all.

Controlling the ball

A skilful first touch gives a player time and space in which to move with the ball or find the best pass. Players who let the ball run away from them are always under pressure to recover control of the ball. This allows time for opponents to close them down, and often means they lose control of the ball completely.

There are a number of ways of controlling the ball, depending on the situation the player is in and the part of the body they use.

Foot control

Control with the foot when receiving the ball requires a soft touch. The technique is simply to withdraw the foot on contact with the ball, often referred to as 'cushioning the ball'. The amount of cushion depends on how quickly the ball is coming. Players should move to the ball, not wait for it to come to them, and keep their eyes firmly on the ball.

The inside of the foot is the safest and most common technique for receiving the ball. It allows the ball to be taken on the move, whereas the old-fashioned method of trapping the ball with the sole (underneath) of the foot involves stopping the ball dead. In a match context, stopping the ball can give the opposition time to get into good defensive positions and/or time to put pressure on the player with the ball and to tackle. Receiving the ball with the top of the foot and outside of the foot are more difficult skills, but the principles of relaxing and withdrawing the foot on impact are the same.

Coaching tips

Receiving the ball (under-sevens)

- On receipt of the ball, relax the receiving foot so the ball stops about one step away (so you can quickly take one step and strike it).
- Be sure the receiving foot is slightly off the ground – if too low the ball will 'bobble' up. Use the arch of the foot to cushion the ball.
- If you want the ball to go to the left or right (instead of straight in front) you must angle your foot in the direction you want it to go.

Receiving the ball (eight years and over)

- While waiting to receive a pass, keep your knees slightly bent and stay on the 'balls' of your feet so you are ready to move quickly to either side. If you raise your heels off the ground about half an inch, you are on the balls of your feet.
- When the ball is kicked, quickly notice its direction – is it going to your left or right or straight at you? It is useful to 'bounce' gently from one foot to the other to help you adjust to the direction of the ball and be ready to move in any direction.
- Move towards the ball.
- Stop the ball in front of you or to the left or right, depending on where your opponent is. If an opponent is not close by, cushion the ball so it moves about one step away from you and in the direction you want to go so you can quickly step up to the ball and pass or shoot it.
- If an opponent is close by, try to cushion or 'take' the ball in a direction that rolls it away from your opponent and into an open area, giving you time and space to dribble, pass or shoot.
- Good players can receive and make passes with both feet and without having to think too long and hard about it.

Chest control

Chest control skill in soccer is often required to bring the ball under control from awkward heights. It can be used to pass the ball and drop the ball to the feet, and to deflect the ball through all angles, even behind.

In all chest control skills, the best technique is to present the whole of the chest to the ball, rather than attempting to take the ball sideways on. Naturally, the greater the surface meeting the ball, the more control the player will have. The ball can be deflected to the side by turning the upper body on contact. When passing the ball with the chest, the chest and back are kept rigid. The breastplate, or sternum, is the hard part of the chest and the area used to generate power for a chest pass. Players will use the power and speed of the ball coming to them to rebound it into the path of a teammate. To stop or 'kill' the ball, the chest and back should be relaxed to cushion the ball and angle it down to the feet. This technique can also be used when the ball is bouncing upwards from the ground.

Thigh control

Thigh control is required when the ball arrives at awkward heights above the knee, but too low to head or chest down. The key is to withdraw the thigh on impact, similar to the 'cushion' technique mentioned above. It is also possible to deflect the ball by rotating the thigh and glancing the ball to the side. Only a small nudge is usually necessary to guide the ball, and coaches should encourage players to deflect the ball and turn in one movement. By making the thigh more rigid, a player can knock the ball up in a controlled way for, say, a volley or drilled pass.

Head control

The aim of the controlled header is to drop the ball to the feet as soon as possible. Players should make contact with the ball in the centre of the forehead, and use their whole body as a shock absorber to cushion the ball. In particular, knees should be bent to drop the upper body, and the back should arch on impact. The head must be upwards when the player receives the ball, in order to cushion it. If they try to head the ball down, they will knock it to the ground, but will not be able to take the pace off the ball. Players must let gravity drop the ball to their feet.

Control drills

All the types of control listed above develop with practice and should be introduced regularly to training sessions from a very early age. Here are just a few drills I use for the various age groups.

Football tennis

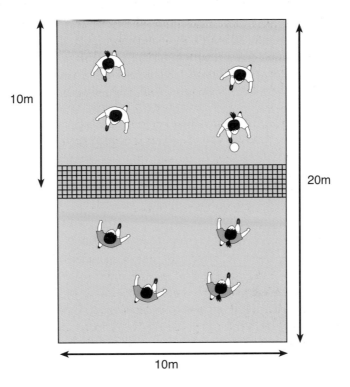

This superb training ground drill incorporates every ball control technique mentioned in this chapter. It is a game designed for players who have developed reasonable skill and control of the ball. You do not need a tennis court – any suitable area will do. For the net, a coach could purchase a garden tennis or badminton net, use two poles with rope and some bibs placed over it, or use the crossbar of a mini or five-a-side goal.

Players have to control the ball at all times in this drill and ensure that the pass over the net keeps the ball on the court and in play. The coach can impose restrictions and rules to help improve certain ball control techniques. For instance, allowing only two touches per player; asking for the ball to be headed over; or specifying that each player in the team touch the ball before it is passed over.

Coaching tip

Keep the teams to a maximum of four against four and have several games going on at once rather than all the players on one big court. This allows all players to stay warm and involved.

Control and shoot

This is another great training ground exercise. It incorporates many techniques and competition for the players, with shot-stopping and angles for the keeper. Players line up on the edge of the 'D'. The goalkeeper kicks or throws a ball in the air to the next player, who has to control the ball using one or more of the techniques and shoot to score from no closer than the penalty spot. The coach can decide how many and which control techniques are used.

The ball can bounce to start with, but as players become more adept they should be encouraged to volley the ball before it touches the ground. As an alternative, the coach, rather than the goalkeeper, can throw in the ball. Ask each player to retrieve any shots that are saved or that go high and wide.

Progression 1 – control and change of direction

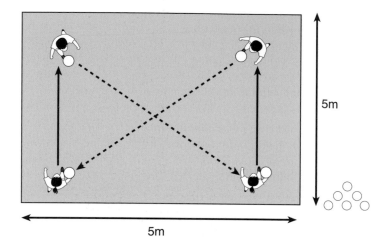

Player one throws the ball to player two who uses a certain ball control technique before passing/volleying to player three to catch. Player three throws the ball to player four who controls the ball before passing/volleying to player one to catch. Rotate the throwers so everyone has a go. This teaches control and change of direction.

Progression 2 – control, pass and move

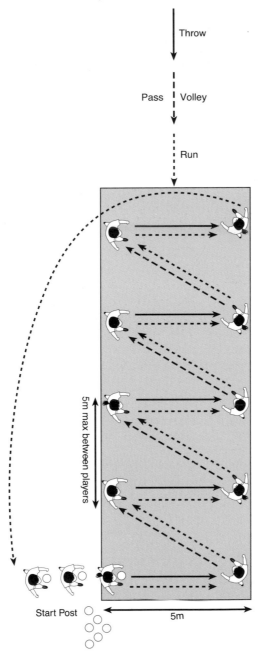

If the team is particularly good at ball control you can join groups to have all players working in one session. Introduce a second and third ball to ensure none of the players get cold and they are always working with a ball. Each player takes the place of the player they have just thrown the ball to or volleyed to. The last player runs round the square to position one and starts the process again. Remember, you must have two or more players at the starting post. Play for two minutes before a minute's rest and recovery break.

Turning

Once players have received the ball and controlled it, they need to move off with it as fast as possible before an opponent can challenge them. They improve their chances of doing this effectively if they can turn quickly and sharply, so it is worth coaching your team in several turns to outwit your opponents. These should be adapted for left-footed players. Get your young players to practise these turns as often as possible – in the garden, in the playground, in games – so that they take responsibility for their progress.

Coaching tip

When players practise turns there are three major do's:

- Start slowly
- Bend knees
- Accelerate away

For the following techniques, set up a square to an appropriate size for the number of players you are coaching. A good guideline is 3 m × 3 m per player. Give all the players a ball and ask them to move around the square practising the moves and turning techniques that the coach calls out. Work for about two minutes on each technique. Finish the exercise by allowing the players to use any turning technique they choose.

Turning away

A player receives the ball and tries to turn immediately and take off in another direction. If they keep running in the same direction, it is too easy for an opponent to guess where the ball will go next, allowing the opponent to catch and attempt to tackle them. The player reaches and hooks to turn the ball, trying not to run around the ball. They work on moving the ball on the turning touch back in the direction they want to go. A good drill for practising this is for two players to pair up 10 metres apart, each with a ball. The players move with the ball towards each other, and as they get closer they turn and move away again.

The outside hook

This is a simple technique to teach and learn. To begin the turn, a player reaches across the body and hooks the ball at the bottom with the outside of their foot. They sweep the ball around to the side with the same foot, leaning in the direction they want to go. The player turns to follow the path of the ball and accelerates away from their opponent as quickly as possible. They must not run around the ball. The ball is moved on the turning, touching it well in front of them and back in the direction they want to go.

The inside hook

As a player receives the ball, they watch out for approaching opponents and lean in the direction they want to go. The shoulder is dropped so that the player is partly turned. Then they hook the inside of the foot around the ball and move off at a sharp angle, dragging the ball with them and accelerating away.

The drag back

This is an ideal technique if a player is being closely marked. The player draws their leg back as if they were about to kick the ball, but swing their foot over it instead. As they bring the leg back again, they catch the top of the ball with their studs and drag the ball back, beginning to spin on their other foot. The player leans in the direction they want to go. When they have pulled the ball back, they complete the turn and accelerate away from their opponent.

The Maradona turn

The Maradona turn, one of the most exciting skills in the game, is named after the great Argentinian soccer star, Diego Maradona. In this technique, the player steps on the ball with one foot and, as they come off the ball, swivel and drag the ball with the other foot. Their momentum will carry the ball with them, allowing them to continue to move forwards.

The Cruyff turn

This technique is named after the Dutch international, Johan Cruyff. This turn and other turning skills should form an essential part of any soccer coaching programme. In the Cruyff turn, the ball is played between the legs, so that it ends up on the opposite side to that expected by the defender. With the ball on their right foot, the player positions themselves as if they were going to turn to the left, or to pass or cross the ball to the left. Then the player flicks the ball between their legs, and makes a quick turn to gather the ball. Usually, if they are using the right foot to send the ball behind them, they will turn in on their left side. The turn should be a quick pivot.

Throw-ins

Throw-in techniques and tactics are some of the more neglected skills in football. With the correct technique, effective training drills and some tactical awareness, a team can make much better use of throw-in opportunities during a game.

The throw-in technique starts by gripping the ball firmly but comfortably. The ball is brought back over the head, and the back is arched. Using the full extent of the arms and the power of the back and shoulders, the ball is released *in front of* the head. The feet position is a matter of personal preference with some players standing square and others placing one foot in front of the other. The final ingredient is to add a short run to generate rhythm and momentum.

Throw-in tactics depend on where the throw is being taken from. In the attacking third of the pitch, the objective is to get the ball into the penalty area as soon as possible, either by a direct throw or by creating an opening for a cross. In the middle third, the tactic should be to make forward runs. In the defensive third, the team must play safe, and try to create space to clear the ball away from danger. Useful tactics for creating space are overlapping runs, sudden changes of direction and decoy runs. A decoy run could take a marker away from the player who would like to receive the throw.

Coaching tip – the basic throw-in

- Stand facing the field with feet apart.
- Place one hand on each side of the ball but slightly behind the ball and form a 'W' with your fingers well spread.
- Take the ball behind the head and throw forwards onto the field.

Remember:

- Both feet must stay on the ground.
- Players can stand on or behind the side line.
- The ball must go behind the head.
- Players must use both hands equally.
- Beginners should throw towards the other team's goal.

A good way to practise throw-ins is to line your team up in a row shoulder-to-shoulder and get them to practise their form without a ball. On the word 'go', they should all pretend to make a throw-in while you watch. Comment and get them to do it again. Be sure they drag the toe of their rear foot, that their hands go behind their head and that they are upright and follow through with both arms.

When coaching throw-ins, look out for these common mistakes:

- Lifting a foot off the ground before the ball has left your hands (this is why it is important to drag the toe of the rear foot).
- Using one hand too much (the assistant referee can call this if it is obvious or if there is a lot of sidespin on the ball).
- Not taking the ball behind the head.

Positional play

When looking at coaching basic skills, it is also worth mentioning how to play in the key positions in football:

- Goalkeeper
- Defender
- Attacker

Goalkeeping basics

All players should have the opportunity to develop goalkeeping skills, particularly the six to nine age group. And let them have fun while they are doing it.

Most young children see the goalkeeper's role as one of being on the goal line, stopping the shots. And they are right! Positional skills, such as narrowing the angle or coming off the line to field a crossed ball, can be encouraged but only once a budding goalkeeper has got the basics right. Children up to the age of 10 are not yet ready for that level of goalkeeping.

Catching the ball

The first skill that young players usually find difficult is catching the ball in the correct fashion. The keeper should always present both palms of the hands outwards to the incoming ball in a 'W' formation. This catching technique is unique to soccer goalkeeping and is the place to start their coaching.

Diving

A soccer goalkeeper needs a specific diving technique, unlike that of any other sport or gymnastic movement. Initially, most players will be reluctant to dive, so a graduated progression is needed. Everything will turn out fine in the end because we know children love to tumble and fall.

Throwing

Throwing a soccer ball is not easy for children with small hands and a lack of strength, especially if the wrong type and size of ball is used. I recommend a size three for children up to 10 years of age and a size four ball for those aged 10 to 14. Never use the size five ball before someone reaches 15 years of age. Throws should be underarm if played short, or from behind the shoulder (overarm) if looking to get distance quickly. The ball should be protected with the hand behind it when throwing.

Kicking

Kicking is invariably a problem for young goalkeepers. They very seldom get distance, and it often takes years of practice to get the timing and co-ordination right, especially for drop-kicks. It is simply a case of practice makes perfect.

What coaches should avoid, particularly in mini soccer, is always getting the 'big lad' with the big kick to take the goal kicks. Simply try and coach your goalkeeper to play safe. Coach the team to accommodate the inability of the goalkeeper to kick long. Perhaps this means coaching your defenders to move wide for a short pass.

Organising

It is important to encourage young goalkeepers to be the eyes and ears of the rest of the team. They have a full view of the pitch and can see the actions, movements and runs of players. This means goalkeepers can issue instructions to their teammates that will help shut down attacks against the team or create a quick counter-attack. The basic message is to teach goalkeepers early on that they should be talking throughout the game in a positive way to their teammates.

Additionally, coaches should encourage goalkeepers to communicate clearly and concisely with their teammates. Goalkeepers should shout loudly but positively if they want the ball cleared or if they are confident that they will catch, kick or receive the ball. A simple instruction of 'away' or 'keeper's ball' is normally sufficient.

Goalkeeping drills

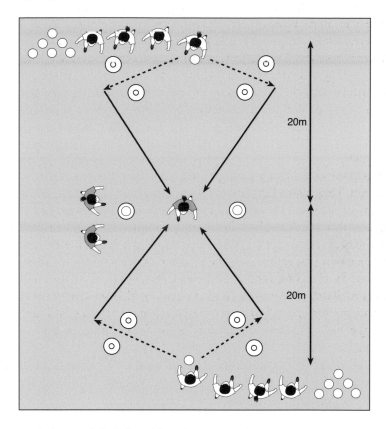

One particularly good drill for older players (aged nine and upwards) is to place two pylons or cones as a goal in the middle of the training square. Have two sets of players each side of the goal, 15–20 metres away. Rotating the strikers from each side, get them to knock the ball out of their feet and strike at goal. Once the shot has been made, a player from the opposite side does the same. In this drill the goalkeeper sees plenty of action and is thoroughly warmed up. To progress, get the strikers to take the ball wide through the cones to practise shooting from wide angles. This also allows the goalkeeper to practise positional skills.

NOTE: Change the goalkeeper after six or eight shots. If you have only one goalkeeper, let them do one minute of activity then rest for a minute and stretch for 30 seconds.

Defending basics

The main purpose of a defender or defending team is to stop the opponents from attacking. There are many ways to do this, and it should always be remembered that defending starts from the moment the opposition gets the ball.

Jockeying

Jockeying – delaying the opponents – allows teammates to get into stronger positions and stop progress by the opposition. Teamwork is important and it should be the whole team's responsibility to defend when necessary and to win the ball back again.

Closing down opponents

Players must know how to close down an opponent quickly if they are approaching the goal. They must be careful not to close in too quickly or their opponent will use this to their advantage and swerve or dummy their way past them. Encourage players to approach the player with the ball at a controlled speed, sideways on and slightly crouched to improve centre of gravity. Get them to keep their eyes firmly on the ball, not on the opponent. They should be light on their toes to effect a quick adjustment should their opponent change direction. Players must be aware of the calls from supporting teammates – communication is vital when defending.

Interception

Interception is a good way of winning the ball back. This technique requires good anticipation, timing and teamwork. Encourage players to look at the way an opponent is shaping to make a pass and to try to get into a space where the ball is going before it gets there. Players should time their run to try and receive the ball in a way that allows them to carry on with momentum towards the opponent's goal. If teammates are pressuring the opponent with the ball, forcing them to make a hurried pass, then the opportunity to counter-attack is increased and improved.

Clearing the ball

Clearing the ball is a priority for defending, especially from inside the goal area. It is not always possible to find the time or space in the area to control the ball and pick out an accurate pass to a teammate, so a quick clearance is the only option. The priority for clearing the ball, whether it be a kick, a header or a goalkeeper's punch, is to get the ball high, long and wide. This provides the time to regroup and 'get shape back' while putting the ball out of the danger zone.

Playing 'out of defence'

There may be times when players do have time on the ball when defending. This is the perfect opportunity for playing out of defence (counter-attacking) and is a great way to catch the opposition off-guard. On the training ground, work on defenders playing a 'crisp' pass to the feet of attackers, who lay the ball off to supporting midfielders. The midfielders should try and get the ball wide immediately and then continue their run to support the attackers or get on to the end of a cross.

Goalkeepers, too, should look to counter-attack at the first opportunity. A quick throw or an accurate kick can suddenly create a counter-attack.

Marking

Marking is another element of defending that requires regular practice. Man-to-man marking means players pick up responsibility for staying close to a specific opponent throughout the game, staying goal-side of them all the time. The defender seldom allows the opponent to dwell or have time on the ball. This is particularly effective when you know that a particular player is a dangerous 'match-winning' opponent.

Many teams adopt a 'sweeper' system, which theoretically eliminates a one-on-one situation arising in defence. The sweeper, as you would imagine, picks up any 'loose' ball that comes free in the defending area. The sweeper allows the central defender and full backs to concentrate on marking attackers. See which system works best for your team. You may need to adapt your defensive strategy and formation to suit the way the match is going.

Defending corners and free kicks

This is another important element that requires regular practice and good teamwork. These are two of the most dangerous situations for a defending team, and to defend successfully requires discipline and confidence. Players must be alert to the many options their opponents might adopt, such as a short corner, pass into midfield, near and far post cross. Get players to remember the golden rules: be alert, be confident and be first to the ball.

Tackling

Tackling is an essential skill because any team must be able to win the ball. If players cannot tackle, they are left relying on intercepting passes when opponents make a mistake. Tackling allows players to compete for the ball and take the initiative.

Beginners should start with the block tackle before learning the sliding tackle.

The block tackle starts by planting the non-tackling foot firmly on the ground to provide a firm anchor. The inside of the foot is used for tackling, not the toe, and it is important to put the full weight of the body behind the football, and to get the head down over the ball.

As with any tackling skill, timing is crucial. Players should try to tackle when their opponent is off-balance, or lets the football go too far in front of them. This is often called 'showing too much of the ball'. Another good time to tackle is when an opponent looks down at the ball.

The sliding tackle or recovery tackle is an essential soccer skill requiring timing and technique. It is not only defenders who need to be able to tackle. Even forwards should be able to make a sliding tackle. It is best to tackle with the foot furthest from the ball. This gives extra reach and reduces the chances of giving away a foul. The sliding tackle is best made from a square position with the leg going out to the side rather than straight in front.

Timing is vital, and it takes plenty of practice to get it right. The key factors for any player are to watch the ball carefully, try to anticipate their opponent's move without being distracted, and always to go for the ball. If a player gets a foot on the ball first there is no foul, but if they miss the ball they will give away a free kick or be 'left for dead'.

A drill for the recovery tackle is for one player, acting as winger, to run with the ball down a narrow 'corridor' towards the touchline. They are given a head start over the defender, who chases after them and tries to make a sliding tackle, putting the ball into touch. The winger must try to reach the touchline without being tackled.

Attacking basics

Whenever a team has possession of the ball, they are in attack, whatever the position of play. To play good attacking football, a team must combine all the skills of passing, movement and support in a positive and assertive way. The object is to get into a position to strike at goal as quickly as possible.

These are just some of the fundamentals of good attacking play:

- Good communication
- Supporting the player with the ball
- Making effective runs into space to take defenders away or to receive the ball
- Choosing passes that find teammates
- Using wall passes or one-twos
- Making crossover runs with teammates to make play unpredictable
- Passing crisply and accurately
- Looking to play 'early' passes
- Not being afraid to shoot when the opportunity arises, and making shots accurate

Shooting

Without shooting at goal, players won't score goals; and goals win matches. Shooting is all about good technique, confidence and taking opportunities. Make sure players always have a go if they see an opportunity. Encourage them not to worry that they might miss, but to try to get the shot on target. They should always try and make the goalkeeper 'work' and vary their shots, trying long- and short-range shots, chips and drives. Players should be alert when their teammates shoot – a rebound can always happen. Shots should be low and aimed for bottom corners away from the goalkeeper.

chapter 7

GAMES

Having introduced basic skills to young players in a structured manner, we now need to see them express themselves in live activity. The best way for a coach to see a child's development, and for the child to show off their new-found skills, is in a fun game situation. This chapter provides coaches with some ideas for introducing lively and fun games into a coaching session. The games are progressive so that each moves on to another, more technical one, or a game that extends their skills.

The one-hour coaching session agenda:

- Warm up with a ball (10 minutes)
- Coach a basic skill (15 minutes)
- Introduce a fun game that allows players to use the new skill (10 minutes)
- Play small-sided games that involve all the players (20 minutes)

With registration and drinks breaks, your packed, hour-long session will fly by.

Fun games that teach skills

NOTE: Some of the games listed are 'knockout' games where the last player left is the winner. Since the first ones knocked out are often the ones who need the most practice, those knocked out should be required to do something either to get back into the game or to keep them working on their ball skills until the game is over. One way round this that I find particularly effective is to let them become the chasers, or an equally important job in the drill. Games are grouped into skills categories with each game teaching players a new aspect of soccer, such as dribbling, juggling and passing.

'The coach says' (5–7 years)

Purpose
To encourage children to run with the ball, keeping it close to their feet.

Area needed
20 m × 20 m.

Action
When the coach says 'Stop – foot on the ball' (or replaces 'foot' with 'knee', 'sit' or 'elbow') the children must do so straight away. The coach can also integrate commands such as change direction, go faster and so on. No one is eliminated from the game.

Equipment
Eight cones to mark area and one ball per child.

Organisation
Mark out a 20 m × 20 m area using the cones. The coach should start by demonstrating what each command means and ensure that all players understand

these. Ask each child to dribble around the area with the ball remaining close to the foot.

Progression

The children have begun the process of dribbling. The next step would be to encourage them to use their peripheral vision. The next drill, 'beware the tiger', will help this.

'Beware the tiger' (8 years and over)

Purpose

To encourage children to look up while dribbling at speed, using their peripheral vision in a controlled, pressurised and fun situation.

Area needed

20 m × 20 m (for around 10 players).

Action

One child volunteers to be the tiger who prowls the jungle (the area) and tries to kick the football away from one of the other jungle animals and into the swamp (outside the area). If the tiger kicks a ball into the swamp, the tiger can retrieve it and become a different jungle animal with a ball. The child whose ball was kicked away is now the tiger.

Equipment

Eight cones and a soccer ball for each child except the Tiger.

Organisation

Set out a 20 m × 20 m area with the cones. Ask the jungle animals to dribble around the jungle, without dribbling into each other or the swamp (the area outside the grid). Remind children of safety points regarding challenging for the ball.

Progression

The next coaching technique would be to change speed and direction while beating a defender. The following game, 'crabs on the beach', will help to illustrate how to develop these techniques in a fun environment.

'Crabs on the beach' (5–8 years)

Purpose

To encourage children to dribble with the ball and change speed and direction to beat an opponent. The art of 'feinting a dummy' can be introduced at this stage.

Area needed

30 m × 20 m grid.

Action

Each child assumes the name of a sea creature, except the crab. Each creature has to run from the beach to the sea with a ball, avoiding the crabs who are trying to 'pinch' the balls. A child whose ball is pinched then becomes a crab.

Equipment

Six cones and a football for each child except the crab.

Organisation

Set out a 30 m × 20 m area with the cones. Make one 30 m line the sea and the other 30 m line the beach. Ask the children (sea creatures) to stand on the beach line, each with a foot on the ball. Place a child (the crab) in the middle of the area.

On the coach's command, tell the creatures to dribble their ball from the beach to the sea while avoiding the crab. When they reach the sea line they must wait with a foot on the ball until all players have crossed the beach. The crab must aim to kick each child's football out of the grid via the 20 m sidelines. Any creatures losing their ball become a crab. The game continues on the coach's command with players now returning from the sea back to the beach. The last three children to be dribbling their footballs become 'sea champs'.

'Numbers' or 'Colours' (6 years and over)

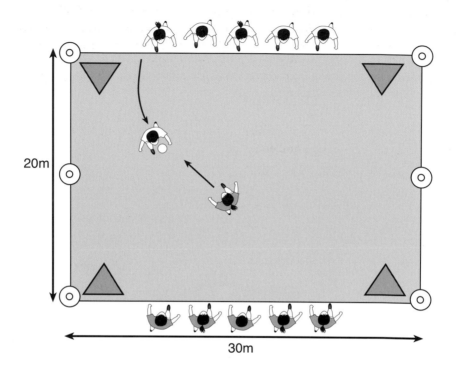

Purpose
To encourage children to be confident to dribble in a one-against-one situation. This game is especially good on a hot day as the children defending can rest a bit.

Area needed
30 m × 20 m grid.

Equipment
Six cones, four pylons or poles as goalposts and a football.

Organisation
Set out a 30 m × 20 m area with the cones. Divide the children into two groups. If you have 12 children, say, assign each child a number between one and six so that each team has a number one, a number two, and so on. Try to make sure the

children with the same number are evenly matched. Set up two very wide 'goals' with pylons. Spread six children on each side across each goal line. Call out one or more numbers, and those children come out to play one against one, two against two and so on. The rest of the children stay spread across the goal line as defenders. Throw a ball from the sideline into the centre and let them play it until a goal is scored or it goes out of bounds. If the opposing team gains possession of the ball, they become the attackers.

TIP: You could use two each of different coloured bibs, as younger children may have trouble remembering numbers.

'Man in the middle' (5 years and over)

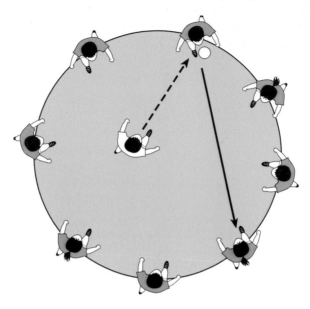

Purpose
To encourage children to shut the ball down and make the correct passing decision.

Area needed
A circle of players relevant to age and numbers.

Equipment
A football.

Organisation
All players form a circle. One player goes in the centre – this can be the coach if working with very young children (*see* tip below). The players forming the circle pass one ball among them while the person in the centre tries to gain control of the ball. When this happens, the last player on the outside to touch the ball goes to the centre. Some level of competitiveness develops but never on an individual basis. Do not allow the player in the middle to work for more than 30 seconds.

TIP: The coach may want to go in the centre to start with but only to intercept a pass, never to tackle. This encourages players, especially the very young ones, to select a correct pass, and the coach can guide them by making it obvious. Make the circle tighter, relative to the players' ability. Sixteen-year-olds and above can play this on a one-touch basis.

Progression
Add a second or third defender in the middle to encourage greater speed of thought, decision, control and passing.

'Monster' (6–8 years)

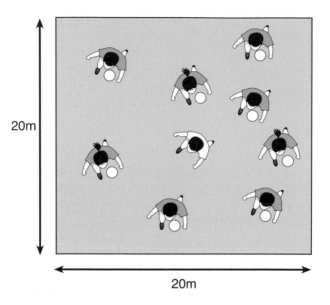

Purpose
Ball control and protecting the ball.

Area needed
20 m × 20 m.

Equipment
Eight cones to mark the area, a football for each player (except the monster) and a coloured bib.

Organisation
Mark off a 20 m × 20 m area for the game to be played and select one player to be the 'monster'. Get the rest of the children (each with a ball) to dribble around within the area. The monster attempts to touch each player on the shoulder or arm, at which point that player 'freezes' with their foot on the ball. If a player's ball goes out of bounds, they also freeze. The last remaining unfrozen player gets to be the new monster for the next round.

'Kick out' (6–8 years)

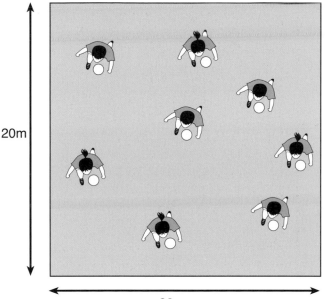

Purpose
Ball control and protection.

Area needed
20 m × 20 m.

Equipment
A football for each player.

Organisation
Everyone dribbles and shields their ball within the area while trying to kick everyone else's ball out, and simultaneously protect their own. Players cannot kick someone else's ball out if their ball is not in the area. If their ball goes out they have to leave the area until it gets down to two children in a duel.

TIP: This game can end quite quickly, which is good for those eliminated early. However, the coach may need to reduce the area to achieve a quick ending.

'Give and go' (8 years and over)

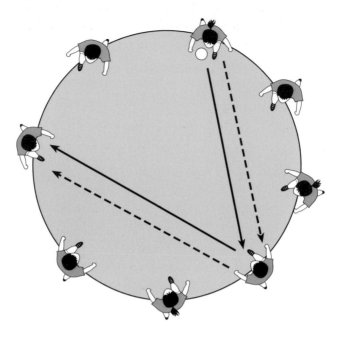

Purpose
This is good for getting the children to move after they make a pass.

Area needed
A circle of players, size depending on numbers, age and ability.

Equipment
One ball (minimum) and a distinctive coloured bib.

Organisation
Get the players to form a circle. Give the ball to one player and they call out someone's name and pass to them. They then run to the receiver's position in the circle. The receiver, on hearing their name called, steps forwards to receive the pass and shouts their own name. The sequence is then repeated. Calling their own name out loud addresses the problem of players thinking someone else is getting the ball or pass. Players also learn each other's names quickly.

TIP: If the same players are involved and others left out, consider starting a countdown from 10 to 0 and get the players to figure out who has been left out (the left out person should be quiet). They start yelling among themselves to figure out who it is, and this fosters communication on the field (it is pretty humorous too).

Progression
Once the players have grasped the game and the quality is improving, throw a second ball into the centre. The players now have to think a bit more because two people are moving and two are busy with the balls.

'Simply score' (6 years and over)

Purpose

To encourage children to shoot at goal and to gain greater appreciation of hitting the target rather than hitting a ball hard.

Area needed

An area appropriate in size to the age, ability and number of players; often this will be the goal area.

Equipment

More footballs than number of players, a goal and cones to mark the shooting line. If you decide to split the group into two teams in competition, bibs will be required.

Organisation

Mark a line 20 m from goal where players line up and a line of cones 5m from goal to shoot from. Get the players to line up across one end of the area. Spread the balls out in front of them. Blow the whistle and turn the players loose. The object of the game is to get all the balls into the net as quickly as possible. They are all on the same team, and are not allowed to take a ball away from another player. Once a player has scored they turn and go back for another ball. Time them to see how fast they can accomplish the task. The children really like this game because they get to score a goal. The more balls the better.

TIP: Players must shoot from behind a line about 5m from goal. This stops players going into the goal and risking being hit by another shot.

'Marbles' (6 years and over)

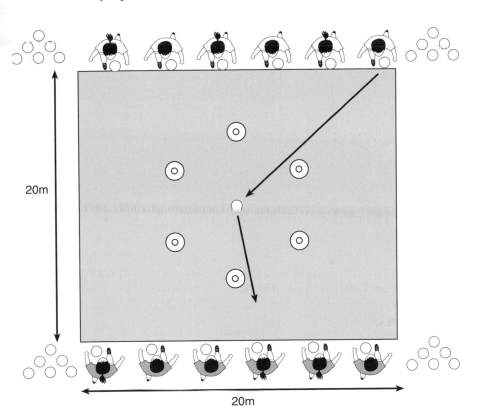

Purpose
To improve accuracy of passing.

Area needed
A rectangle appropriate in size to the age, ability and number of players.

Equipment
More footballs than players, a distinctive coloured football as the marble, cones to mark the centre area and the touchlines.

Organisation

Split your team into two groups and line them up behind two opposing lines, 20 m apart. Each player should have a ball. Place an unusual coloured (or size) ball in the middle. This is the marble (a size two ball works well). Get the players to try to move the marble across the other team's line, or outside the inner circle of cones, by striking it with a ball. After the game starts, players are free to use any ball they can find. At first, the players may get really excited and kick the marble. If this happens, stop the game and put it back. Players must kick their football from behind their base line and use the correct passing style of kick (no toe-punts). The game is over when the ball exits the area.

Variation

Have more than one marble.

'Shark and minnows' (6 years and over)

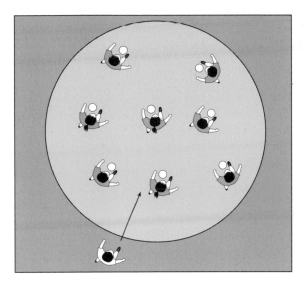

Purpose
This game teaches children with the ball to shield it from an opponent, and teaches children without the ball how to take an opponent's ball.

Area needed
A circle appropriate in size to the age, ability and number of players.

Equipment
A football for all players in the circle and a distinctive coloured bib for the 'shark'.

Organisation
Mark out a circle. One player, the shark, starts outside the circle without a ball. All other players, the minnows, start inside the circle with a ball. When the coach yells, 'Shark's getting hungry!' the shark starts running around the outside of the circle and the fish start dribbling around inside the circle. When the coach yells, 'Shark attack!' the shark enters the circle and has 30 seconds to send as many balls as possible outside the circle. When a ball leaves the circle for any reason, the corresponding fish must leave the circle and stay out until the coach gives the 'Stop!' command at the end of the 30 seconds. A fish has done well if still alive. The shark has done well if very few fish survived. Choose a new shark and play another round until every player has been the shark once. Add competition as you see fit, i.e. which shark can kick most balls away?

'Alamo' (7 years and over)

Purpose
To encourage children to shoot at goal and to gain greater appreciation of hitting the target rather than hitting a ball hard.

Area needed
An area appropriate in size to the age, ability and number of players; often this will be two × corridors 30 m long by 10 m wide.

Equipment
Plenty of footballs on the goal line at each end, two goals, 16 cones to mark the areas, bibs in two colours.

Organisation
Mark two corridors 30 m long × 10 m wide (or as otherwise appropriate) side by side with a goal and a goalkeeper at one end of each corridor (no goalkeeper if players are under eight). Create two teams in different bibs. Line up the teams on opposite ends. They each have a ball. On the whistle, the first two players on each side dribble the ball, make quick passes to a point 5 m from goal and shoot the ball into goal. They then get the ball out of goal and run to the back of the queue coming the other way. Ask players to cheer their teammates. This can be a good team competition by adding up each team's score.

'Explode' (6 years and over)

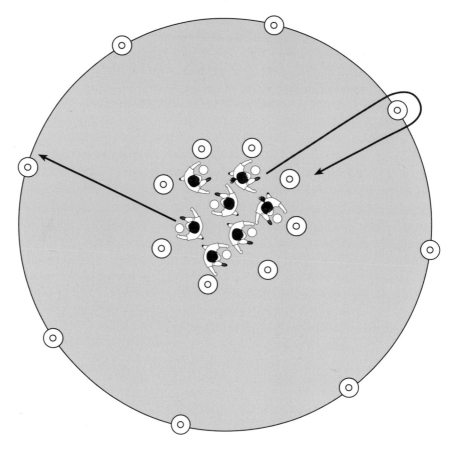

Purpose
To encourage children to maintain control of their ball at pace.

Area needed
Two circles of cones – one inner and one outer – size relevant to age and number of players.

Equipment
A football for each player.

Organisation

Lay out an inner and outer ring of cones. Ask the players to dribble their ball in the inner circle. Make sure they use the insides of both feet. Make them keep control of the ball – always within one step – and do not let them run into one another or dribble their ball into another ball or another player. Keep telling them to keep their heads up and see the open spaces. On the shout 'Explode!' the players all run away (dribbling their balls) as fast as they can. The first one to get to a boundary cone with their foot on the ball and their arm raised is the winner.

Progression

Players explode out, go round an outer cone and run back to the inner circle. The first one back with their foot on the ball and their arm raised is the winner.

'Slalom/dribble relay' (7 years and over)

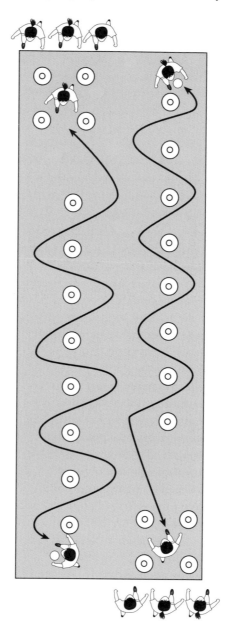

Purpose
Ball control at pace.

Area needed
Two channels of cones in an area 20 m long × 10 m wide. Increase this to 30 m long for players of 11 years and above.

Equipment
Two footballs and 24 cones – 16 for the slaloms and 8 for target 'home' zones.

Organisation
Set up an obstacle course with cones as 'gates'. Split the group into Team A and Team B. Each player takes it in turn to race against a player from the other team. If a player loses control or misses a gate, they have to regain control and go back through the gate. The final pass must go to the next player waiting in a target zone. A variation is to have a small 'square' at each end. Players have to stop the ball in the square, then sprint back and 'high-five' the next player before they can take off. Players waiting their turn must stay in the square until their teammate returns. Add more cones and gates as the players improve their dribbling technique and skill.

'Red light/green light' (6–8 years)

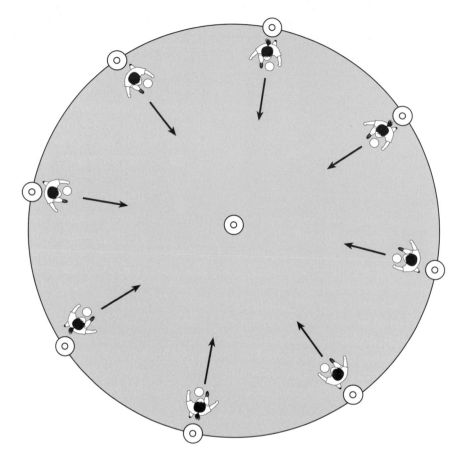

Purpose
To encourage children to dribble with the ball and change speed while retaining control of the ball.

Area needed
A large circle around 30 m in diameter.

Equipment
Cones to mark the outer edge of the circle, a football for each child, a large traffic-type cone or pole.

Organisation

Each player with a ball waits on the edge of a big circle. Place a large traffic cone or pole in the middle as the target. The objective is for the players to dribble their ball to the traffic cone. However, the players can only move when the coach shouts, 'Green light'. The children race across the circle to see who can reach the traffic cone first. After a few seconds, the coach shouts, 'Red light'. At that command the players must stop and put a foot on top of the ball. The coach looks for players whose ball is still moving. Those players must move a certain distance back towards the starting line. Repeat calling red light/green light until someone wins the race by placing their hand on the traffic cone or pole, with their foot on the ball. The coach can add a bit of fun by calling out other words beginning with G or R to trick the players, such as 'Go', 'Get ready', 'Right', 'Ready break' or 'Run'.

'Dribbler's alley' (9 years and over)

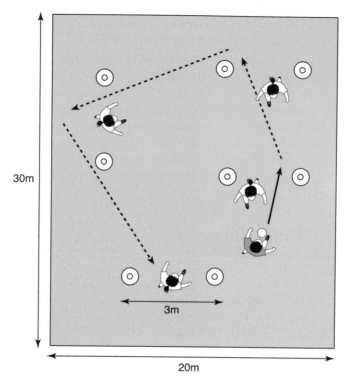

Purpose
To encourage children to dribble past opponents in order to score.

Area needed
30 m × 20 m grid.

Equipment
Six cones to mark the outer area, eight cones to mark four goals and a football for each attacker.

Organisation
You need four or more players. Set up four goals/gates using the cones. Each goal should be 3 m wide, and there should be at least 3–5 m between each one. Each player guards a goal, and the remaining players try to dribble through it. The winner is the player who gets through the most goals without being tackled.

'The hunter' (9 years and under)

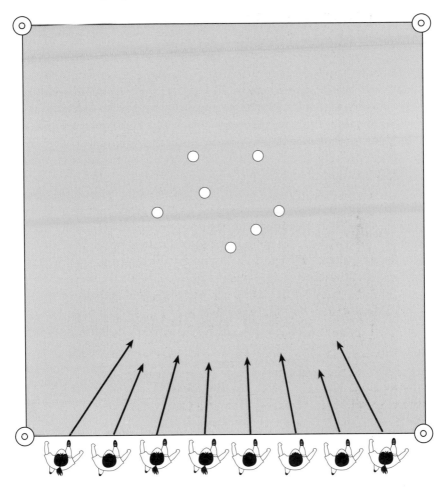

Purpose

To encourage children to dribble with the ball and change speed and direction to beat an opponent. To help them learn the art of protecting their football from others.

Area needed

30 m × 20 m grid.

Equipment
Cones to mark the area of play. One football fewer than the number of players.

Organisation
In this high-activity game, all players stand at a cone about 6m from a group of balls. There is one ball fewer than the number of players. On the coach's command, the players run to the balls, get one and begin dribbling within a grid. The player who does not get a ball becomes the hunter and tries to steal one from the others. After a preset period has passed, the coach stops the game. The player who does not have a ball at that time is the hunter.

Progression
Place the balls at the far end of the playing area with the players lined up on the opposite line. On the coach's command, the players race to retrieve a ball and try to return to the start line without being tackled by the hunter. If the hunter 'steals' a ball from the other player, the player dispossessed becomes the hunter. Play stops when all the players with a ball are back on the start line with their foot on the ball and an arm raised. Add competition by seeing who is the best hunter in the team. Ensure that all players get an opportunity to be hunters.

'Tag' (7 years and over)

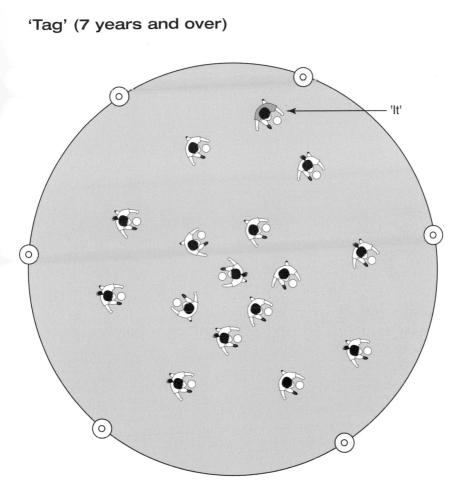

'It'

Purpose
Maintaining control of the ball while under pressure.

Area needed
Large circle or square, maximum 40 m × 40 m.

Equipment
Cones to mark the outer edge of the playing area. A football for everyone.

Organisation

This drill is based on the common children's game of tag. Mark off a grid or circle. Everybody needs a ball. One player volunteers to be 'it'. Whoever is 'it' must dribble to another player and tag them. The other player avoids being tagged by dribbling away from 'it'. If the player being chased loses their ball outside the grid, dribbles out of the grid or is tagged, they become 'it' and the game continues.

Progression

'Ball tag'. Everyone has a ball and dribbles in a confined area. The player who is 'it' must pass their ball so that it hits another player's ball. The player whose ball is hit then becomes 'it' but cannot hit the ball of the player who has just hit their ball.

'Snake' (6–8 years)

Purpose
To teach co-ordination, teamwork and basic ball control skills.

Area needed
40 m × 40 m.

Equipment
Four cones to mark out the area. A football for each group of three.

Organisation
Players are grouped into threes (preferred) or fours. The first player is the 'head' of the snake and does not have a ball. They are the leader in a follow-the-leader game. The second player is the 'body' and has a ball at their feet, and must follow the head of the snake, dribbling wherever they go. The third player is the 'rattle' without a ball and just following. Encourage the 'heads' to vary their lead by moving fast, slow, sideways and stopping. I let one player lead for about 20 seconds. Then, on a whistle from the coach, player two leaves the ball for player three and becomes the head of the snake. Player three becomes the body and the former head of the snake circles around to become the rattle.

'Decision time' (8 years and over)

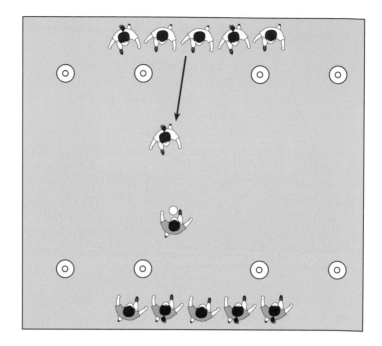

Purpose
To develop confidence in taking on and beating an opponent.

Area needed
20 m × 20 m.

Equipment
Eight cones to create four goals. Six footballs.

Organisation
Place two small goals on one side of a grid and two goals opposite. Split the players into two groups and give them a number: one, two, three and so on. The coach throws a ball into the centre and calls out a number. The corresponding players play one against one, trying to score through either of the opponent's goals. This can be a competitive team game – first player or team to five or ten goals.

'Circle game' (6 years and over)

Side line

Side line

Goal line

Purpose

Keeping control of the football under pressure.

Area needed

30 m × 30 m square with an inner circle of cones.

Equipment

Four cones to mark the area of play plus enough cones to mark an inner circle. A football for all players.

Organisation

Set up a grid, from 20 m × 20 m to 30 m × 30 m in size, depending on age, ability and number of players, make a centre circle and split players into two teams that can be identified by a colour. Get all the players to dribble their balls in the centre circle. Call out a colour. That team dribbles towards their goal line. The players in the other team leave their balls and run to slow the attackers down, trying to get them to a sideline and to dribble out-of-bounds, or not get to their goal line before the coach counts to seven. Coaches should award a point for each out-of-bounds and a point for each player 'held' for the coach's count. Attackers get a point for each player who gets the ball to their goal line. Play to 10 or 20 points depending on the ability of your players.

'Keeping the ball' (6 years and over)

Purpose
Keeping control and protecting the ball.

Area needed
20 m × 20 m.

Equipment
Four cones to mark the area. A football for all players.

Organisation
Everyone dribbles around, trying to keep their own ball and kick out everyone else's ball. If a player's ball is kicked out, they must retrieve it then toe-tap or box-the-ears of the ball for 10 touches before getting back in. A player gets a point for every ball they kick out (so if you spend time outside dancing on your ball, you have less time to win points).

'Maps' (8 years and over)

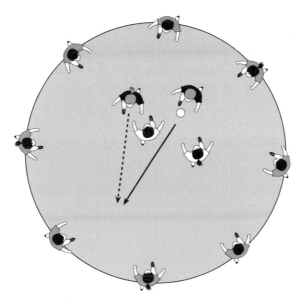

Purpose
This drill teaches awareness of Movement, Availability, Pace and Space – MAPS.

Area needed
Circle of players, the size dependent on numbers, ability and ages.

Equipment
One football and four bibs in two different colours.

Organisation
Players form a circle. One of the players on the outside has the ball. Four players work inside the circle, two designated as attackers and the other two as defenders. To start, an attacker in the centre calls for a pass from the player on the outside with the ball. The attacker looks to control the ball and pass to their teammate or another player on the outside but not the player they received the first pass from. An attacker then moves to a position where they can receive the ball and play continues. The defenders try to dispossess the attacker and, if successful, become the attacker. Play for a maximum of a minute then swap the players with players on the outside. The drill teaches players many aspects of the game such as effective movement, creation of space, receiving the ball, taking defenders 'away', passing techniques, decision-making and good ball control.

Ball juggling: 'P-E-L-E' (8–11 years)

Purpose
To practise ball skills in pairs.

Area needed
Enough room to work with the ball.

Equipment
Each player needs a football (although two players can share one).

Organisation
Divide the team into pairs. The first player keeps the ball up once using a part of the body. The second player has to mirror this. The first player then juggles twice, and the second player matches. The first player then juggles three times, and so on. When a player misses, the other player gets a letter: first 'P' then 'E' then 'L' then 'E'. After awarding a letter, the players start out at one again. The first player to spell PELE is the winner. This can be played with thighs only, feet only, head only or any combination.

'The juggler' (7–11 years)

Purpose
To practise ball skills in pairs.

Area needed
Enough room to work with the ball.

Equipment
Each player needs a football (although two players can share one).

Organisation
Play with two or more players. The first player keeps the ball up with as many touches as they can and keeps track of count. The second player goes after the first miss. After the second player misses, the first player goes again, resuming the count from where they missed in their first turn. For example, if a player got five touches in their first turn, they would start the second turn at six. The first player to a specific number wins.

Progression
This game can be made more challenging by restricting it to certain body parts. For more experienced and skilful players who can keep the ball up with hundreds of touches, you can have both players working at the same time, counting out loud the number of touches they have. The winner is the first one to reach a certain number.

'Juggling with movement' (9 years and over)

Purpose
Ball control on the move.

Area needed
Enough distance to move with the ball.

Equipment
One football (but the more the better) and a goal/target.

Organisation
Players start at one spot and walk/jog/run while juggling the ball (no hands!). The aim is for players to see how far they can go without dropping the ball. A variation of this is to start at the outside of the penalty area on the field, juggle up to the goal area and shoot/volley the ball into the net without letting it hit the ground.

Progression
You could have a race between two more experienced and skilful players, or time them between two points before they shoot.

'Timed juggles' (9–11 years)

Purpose
To see how many touches the player can get in a certain amount of time.

Area needed
Enough area to juggle a football.

Equipment
One football.

Organisation
Do a two-minute timed contest. Initially the players do not have to keep the ball up without a miss. This is great for getting the players focused and working hard for a certain time period. It's also good for aerobic fitness.

'Team juggling contest' (7–11 years)

Purpose
To see how many touches a team can get in a certain amount of time.

Area needed
Enough for all players to line up and juggle a football facing their opponents.

Equipment
One football for each player.

Organisation
Get each player to juggle and see how many touches they can get. Add the total touches for the whole team and create a team record. When the players are not very good jugglers, this game does not take very long. I have seen huge improvements in my teams' juggling skills by doing nothing more than this game. It is just enough focus to get them working on their own. Very young players can catch the ball at times. Ensure you ask them to practise at home and try to beat their record.

'Keeper wars' (8 years and over)

Purpose
Goalkeeper warm-up.

Area needed
5–10 m long × 5 m wide.

Equipment
Four cones to create two goals, lots of footballs for both keepers.

Organisation
Using four cones, create two goals about 5–8 m apart (depending on players' age, ability and so on). The width of the goals should be just beyond the armspan of the keepers. The keepers sit just in front of the cones, facing each other. Each attempts to score goals by throwing the ball through the opponent's goal. The ball must be kept below their shoulders.

'Goalkeeper rotations'

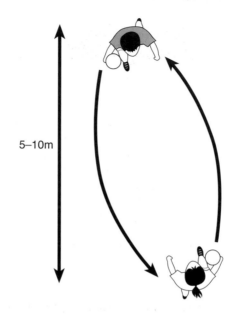

5–10m

Purpose
Goalkeeper warm-up.

Area needed
5 m × 5 m.

Equipment
Two footballs of any size.

Organisation
Two goalkeepers face each other, both with a ball. Using the right hand, they throw their ball to the other keeper and continue the rotation, speeding up as they become more comfortable with the requirements of the game. Start each goalkeeper with, say, five points. The first one to drop their ball loses a point until there is a winner. Take a break, then start again using the left hand. Other variations include high and wide throws. You can also use a standard-size ball and a tennis ball to encourage alertness and flexibility.

'Penalty king' (8 years and over)

Purpose

To boost confidence, improve accuracy of shooting and goalkeeper's positioning and reflexes.

Area needed

The goal area; 10 m × 10 m up to 20 m × 20 m, depending on age and ability of the players.

Equipment

Minimum two players (one goalkeeper), one goal, five footballs (minimum), one cone or pole.

Organisation

Place the goalkeeper on the goal line and the ball on the penalty spot. Place a cone or pole 5–10 m back from the ball. On the word 'Go' the goalkeeper runs around a goal post or touches it and prepares themselves to save the penalty while the striker turns and runs around the pole, and then strikes the ball. This continues without stopping for five penalties. To add competition, the striker only wins if they score three goals or more. Make sure you swap the goalkeepers and players regularly so they can rest and have a drink.

'Strike to score' (9 years and over)

Purpose
Encourages passing, control, shooting and shot-stopping.

Area needed
18-yard area.

Equipment
Plenty of footballs, goal and four cones.

Organisation
Place a 10 m × 10 m square marked by cones inside the penalty area on the corner of the 18-yard area. Have a stock of footballs outside the penalty box on the other side at the corner of the 18-yard area. Player one by the footballs passes a football to player two in the grid who controls with their first touch and strikes at goal with their second touch. To encourage a good first touch the ball cannot leave the grid. Player two now moves to the bunch of footballs while player one goes around the goal to retrieve any shots and joins the group of strikers in the grid. Goalkeepers can take it in turn to stop the shot. The winner is the first player to score a certain number of goals or the goalkeeper to stop a certain number of shots.

appendix 1

useful addresses

ChildLine
Freepost III
London N1 0BR
Tel: 0800 1111
Website: www.childline.org

Coachwise (information on coaching
qualifications, plus resources and
reference material)
Chelsea Close
Off Amberley Road
Armley
Leeds LS12 4HP
Tel: 0113 201 5555
Website: www.1st4sport.com
Email: enquiries@1st4sport.com

FA Premier League
30 Gloucester Place
London W1U 8PL
Website: www.premierleague.com
Email: contactus@premierleague.com

The Football Association (FA)
25 Soho Square
London W1D 4FA
Website: www.thefa.com

Football Conference
51 Highfield Road
Dartford DA1 4HG
Tel: 01322 292199
Website:
www.footballconference.co.uk

The Football Foundation
30 Gloucester Place
London W1U 8FF
Tel: 0845 345 4555
Website: www.footballfoundation.org
Email: enquiries@footballfoundation.
org

Football League
30 Gloucester Place
London W1U 8PL
Tel: 0870 4420 1888
Website: www.football-league.co.uk
Email: fl@football-league.co.uk

**The Independent Football
Commission**
Victoria Court
82 Norton Road
Stockton-on-Tees TS18 2DE
Tel: 0870 060 1610
Website: www.theifc.co.uk
Email: contact@theifc.co.uk

NSPCC National Centre
42 Curtain Road
London EC2A 3NH
Tel: 020 7825 2525
Website: www.nspcc.org.uk
NSPCC hot line: 0808 800 5000

Sports Coach UK (formerly The National Coaching Foundation)
114 Cardigan Road
Headingly
Leeds LS6 3BJ
Tel: 0113 274 4802
Website: www.sportscoachuk.org
Email: coaching@sportscoachuk.org

Sport England
3rd floor Victoria House
Bloomsbury Square
London WC1B 4SE
Tel: 08458 508508
Website: www.sportengland.org
Email: info@sportengland.org

Youth Justice Board for England and Wales
11 Carteret Street
London SW1H 9DL
Tel: 020 7271 3033
Website: www.youth-justice-board.gov.uk
Email: enquiries@yjb.gsi.gov.uk

Youth Sports Trust
Sir John Beckwith Centre for Sport
Loughborough University
Loughborough
Leicestershire LE11 3TU
Tel: 01509 228293
Website: www.youthsporttrust.org
Email: info@youthsporttrust.org

All of the following titles have passed the FA Coaches Association (FACA) quality assessment for content and value. To obtain a title, contact the head office in Leeds or the FA in London:

FACA Resources
PO Box 35
Leeds LS12 4XY
Tel: 0113 279 1395
Fax: 0113 231 9606

The FA Resource and Reference Library

To order any of the following resources, please phone the FA National Game Division on 020 7745 4596 or 020 7745 4597, or contact the Football Association, 25 Soho Square, London W1D 4FA. Alternatively, visit the official FA website at www.thefa.com.

Club Development

Charter Standard Club Development Manual
(includes funding booklet, code of good practice booklet, child protection policy and procedures, goalpost safety leaflet and FA resource leaflet)
This is designed to assist progressive clubs plan for their future and work towards becoming an FA-approved Charter Standard Club. The manual is supported by the FA Charter Standard Workshop.

Club Administration Manual
This is designed as an introduction and guide for all those engaged in grassroots football administration, particularly club secretaries.

Setting up a Club
A useful guide for volunteers, football development officers and sports development officers wishing to set up new football clubs.

A Guide to Sponsorship
A must for all grassroots clubs looking to gain sponsorship at a local level.

Volunteer development

Football Workforce Flyer
Provides information on the Football Workforce initiative and how to access the manual and Effective Football Club Administration training programme.

Football Workforce Manual
This supports an important new programme from the FA which recognises the value of volunteers in the development of football at every level. The manual provides practical advice from real volunteers on the recruitment and retention of volunteers.

Effective Football Club Administration (EFCA) Programme
This leaflet provides information on the EFCA training programme, which has been established in conjunction with Sport England, aimed at developing the administration of grassroots football clubs.

Women's and girls' football development

Girls' and Women's Football Development Programme – Good Practice Guide
Contains examples of good practice in the development of the female game at all levels.

Women's and Girls' Football League Development Manual
A resource for administrators, development officers and league officials wishing to develop a new girls' or women's league.

Women's and Girls' Football Poster
Ideal for clubs looking to recruit new members.

Girls' Football Flyers
Ideal for clubs or leagues trying to recruit new members, promote an event or provide information on their organisation.

England Women's Team Squad Postcards and Posters
Available to clubs, leagues, development officers and football in the community schemes, which are running courses or events specifically for girls. Individual postcards of the England women's team manager, Hope Powell, are also available.

Women's Football Video
A promotional tool for development officers, clubs, leagues and community schemes running events, seminars or workshops to promote the development of women's football.

Women's Football Information Wallet
This pack contains factual
information including the history of
the women's game, competitions and
the national team. Ideal for students
to assist with research.

How to Run a Girls' Football Festival
A resource for development officers,
clubs and leagues who are looking to
provide a high-profile event to attract
new girls' teams to take part in a
league or individual players to join a
club.

*How to Run a Girls' Football Mini-
league*
A resource for development officers to
provide competitive opportunities for
girls who live in an area where there
are no teams for them to join, or who
do not yet have the confidence to join
their local team.

*How to Run a Girls' Football School
League*
Advice on good practice when setting
up and running a schools' football
league.

Football development

*Setting up a Coaching Centre – an
Example of Good Practice*
Available to local authorities and
county FAs running FA Coaching
Centres.

*Girls' Football 'Kick Start' Resource
Cards and Planning Pack*
Available to development officers and
coaches involved in the delivery of the
Active Sports Kick Start scheme.

Women's and Girls' Football Newsletter
Up-to-date information and good
practice in the field of women's and
girls' football. If you are a club,
school, league, community officer or
development officer, or just generally
interested in what's going on in the
world of women's and girls' football
development, then make sure you are
on the mailing list for this
informative newsletter.

Women's Football Bulletin
A weekly bulletin bringing you news
from the Women's Premier League,
FA and League Cup, international
round-up and hot-off-the-press news
stories from around the region.

Mini-soccer Handbook
A must for leagues, clubs or
development officers providing mini-
soccer opportunities for girls and
boys, including the laws of the game.

Football Development Certificates
Available to clubs, leagues and
development officers running
promotional events.

*Top Sport Football Community
Guidance Notes*
Available to local authority sports
development officers involved in the
delivery of the Community Top Sport
Football programme.

Goalpost Safety Leaflet
A must for everyone involved in using
football goalposts, to ensure the safety
and welfare of players at all times.

Schools' football

*Charter Standard Schools' Brochure
and Application Form*
Available to any school interested in
achieving the FA Charter Standard
Schools' Award.

Charter Standard Schools' Newsletter
(for information only)
A newsletter specifically for Charter
Standard-accredited Schools,
providing up-to-date information.

*Junior Football Organisers' Resource
Pack* (for information only)
This resource pack is available only to
schools running the FA Junior
Football Organisers' Course for their
students. The pack provides
information on how to deliver safe
and fun football sessions, how to play
and referee mini-soccer matches and
how to plan and implement a festival
or tournament for 6–11-year-olds.

Equity

One-One Ability Counts Leaflet
This leaflet provides information for
Football in the Community schemes
on the One-One Ability Counts
programme managed by the English
Federation of Disability Sport and
supported by the FA. The scheme has
been developed to encourage the
advancement of playing opportunities
for people with disabilities.

Equity Guidelines and Good Practice
These guidelines have been produced
to support the development of
opportunities for everyone to take
part in football at grassroots level.

Coach education

New Generation of Courses Brochure
Information on all the FA coach
education and medical courses
available to potential or existing
coaches.

The FA Coaches Association (FACA)
Application Form
(Automatically provided on receipt of
an FA coaching qualification.)

FACA provides many services to
coaches, including up-to-date
information through its *Insight*
magazine, in-service training
opportunities, insurance cover,
coaching resources booklet
(purchasable items) and an annual
conference to support the education
and development of coaches at all
levels within the game.

Curriculum Guide
(can be purchased via Coachwise –
Tel: 0113 279 1395)
A guide for teachers delivering
football at Key Stages 2, 3 and 4.

The FA Child Protection
Policy/Procedures
A guide for everybody involved in the
delivery or organisation of youth
football.

appendix 3

SAMPLE RISK ASSESSMENT FORM

Risk assessment form

Venue/Date:
Name/position:

Playing/Training Area

Are areas free of dangerous obstacles? Is area fit and appropriate for chosen activity? (Tick appropriate response.)

Yes   No

Outline any hazards and detail what action was taken or will be taken:

Goalposts/other equipment

Are goalposts safe and appropriate for the activity? Yes   No

Outline any unsafe equipment, who may be at risk and what action was taken:

Players

Is the emergency contacts/medical register completed and up-to-date?

Yes   No

Outline current state and what action was taken:

Is all the players' attire appropriate and safe for chosen activity?

Yes   No

Outline any unsafe equipment/attire and any action taken:

Emergency Points

Can emergency vehicles access areas safely and without obstacle?

Is telephone working?

Index

Notes

ALSO AVAILABLE FROM A&C BLACK:

101 Youth Soccer Drills – age 7 to 11 *2nd edition*
101 Youth Soccer Drills – age 12 to 16 *2nd edition*

by Malcolm Cook

The 101 Drills books are the practice bible for youth football coaches. Designed specifically for primary and secondary age groups respectively, each manual contains a wide range of progressive practice drills to help young players develop. Fun, educational and challenging, all drills are illustrated and cover the essential technical skills, including:

* warming up
* dribbling and running with the ball
* passing
* shooting

* heading
* crossing
* warming down

As well as easy-to-use instructions, each drill contains information on the equipment needed, the space required and how to organise the players.

> *'For 30 years, Malcolm Cook has shone his light down the path of soccer development and progress'* **Andy Roxburgh, UEFA Technical Director**

Available in all good bookshops and online. For more information on A&C Black titles, visit www.acblack.com

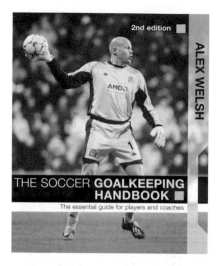

The Soccer Goalkeeping Handbook *2nd edition*

by Alex Welsh

This book is the authoritative and comprehensive coaching guide to the most important position on the football field.

The art of successful goalkeeping depends on sound basic techniques and efficient decision-making. *The Soccer Goalkeeping Handbook* identifies the major components that form the essential skills of any goalkeeper, outlining tried-and-tested practices and training drills to help improve match performance. Topics covered include:

- positioning
- one-on-one situations
- distribution
- dealing with high crosses
- coping with back passes
- shot stopping and improvising saves from deflections

- sweeping up behind the defence and organisation at set pieces
- saving penalties
- building confidence.

Fully updated throughout to include the latest information and advice, it provides essential reading for all experienced and aspiring goalkeepers.

Available in all good bookshops and online. For more information on A&C Black titles, visit www.acblack.com

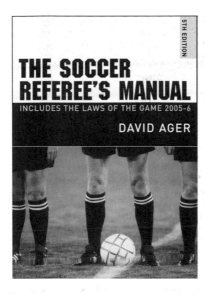

The Soccer Referee's Manual *5th edition*

by David Ager

Written by an acknowledged authority, *The Soccer Referee's Manual* is an invaluable reference guide for referees at all levels of the game, and includes:

- FIFA's Laws of the Game
- guidance on expectations of how referees should administer the laws and control play
- valuable insights into the FA's referee training and advice
- over 100 questions and answers on the laws and their interpretation.

Revised and updated from previous editions, this book continues to deliver the latest guidance on this crucial role on the field.

'An excellent resource for all levels of the game' **The Bulletin of Physical Education**

'Written with such common sense, as well as proper regard for the Laws of the Game, that it should be read by every football player, manager and spectator'
All Sport and Leisure Monthly

Available in all good bookshops and online. For more information on A&C Black titles, visit www.acblack.com